THE
MUSIC LISTENER'S
COMPANION

SECOND EDITION

JAY D. ZORN
University of Southern California

PRENTICE HALL
Englewood Cliffs, New Jersey 07632

Library of Congress Cataloging-in-Publication Data

Zorn, Jay D.
  The music listener's companion / Jay D. Zorn.—2nd ed.
    p.   cm.
  Includes bibliographical references (p.   ) and index.
  ISBN 0-13-097957-0
  1. Concerts. 2. Musicians. 3. Music appreciation. I. Title.
  MT90.Z67   1995
  780—dc20   93-50848
                                                          CIP
                                                          MN

Publisher: *Bud Therien*
Editorial/production supervision: *Margaret Antonini*
Manufacturing buyer: *Robert Anderson*
Cover design: *Design Solutions*

Cover photograph: *JoAnn Falletta, Music Director of The Long Beach
    Symphony. Courtesy of Steve J. Sherman, photographer.*

Printed in the United States of America
10 9 8 7 6 5 4 3 2

ISBN 0-13-097957-0

Prentice-Hall International (UK) Limited, *London*
Prentice-Hall of Australia Pty. Limited, *Sydney*
Prentice-Hall Canada Inc., *Toronto*
Prentice-Hall Hispanoamericana, S.A., *Mexico*
Prentice-Hall of India Private Limited, *New Delhi*
Prentice-Hall of Japan, Inc., *Tokyo*
Simon & Schuster Asia Pte. Ltd., *Singapore*
Editora Prentice-Hall do Brasil, Ltda., *Rio de Janeiro*

CONTENTS

A WORD OF WELCOME

Becoming an informed listener doesn't take years of concertgoing: it takes practical information and a few concert experiences. I wrote this book to de-mystify that information and to make it easy for you to have those experiences.

You've made a good choice. This book can be your all-inclusive guide to the exciting world of classical music and its concert protocol. You will soon be choosing the most enjoyable concerts to suit your tastes and preferences, finding the best seats in the house, reading programs skillfully, making sense of the various styles of music you are likely to hear, recognizing the end of movements and the entire piece, and knowing when to applaud—just as seasoned concertgoers do.

As a performer and conductor myself, I share some personal insights in describing the procedures for various kinds of concerts, as well as the roles and activities of performers, conductors, and guest soloists. You will find guides on musical forms, elements, and structure. You will explore the music of the typically programmed style periods—Baroque, Classical, Romantic, Impressionistic, 20th Century, etc. Once you discover what to listen for in these styles, you will have acquired the foundation of music appreciation.

Based on the success of the first edition and on feedback from readers, this expanded second edition features:

- a new, comprehensive **Directory of Classical Music Radio Stations in Canada and the United States** and those stations which present the **live Metropolitan Opera** broadcasts. (Be sure to take this directory with you on your next trip, and you will know which stations to listen to.)

- an extensive **Suggested Record Library** to help you build your personal collection.

- an in-depth section on **Writing Concert Reports and Research Papers**.

- new charts, graphs, and tables on **Common Music Catalog Designations, Common Tempo Terms and Descriptions, Detailed Music Forms**.

- **Conducting Pattern Diagrams** to help you understand and to try your hand at conducting.

- more detailed **Style Period Descriptions and Summaries**.

Concert lovers with all ranges of experience will enjoy the insights in this practical guide. A lifetime of listening pleasure is at your fingertips. I welcome your comments and feedback.

Dr. Jay Zorn
University of Southern California

ACKNOWLEDGMENTS

With its variety of photographs, concert programs, and illustrations, this book required the assistance of many professionals. I extend my appreciation to

June August
Writer, editor, photographer, writing consultant

Miriam Spiro
Publicist, ICM Artists, LTD.

Francine Di Blasi
Public Relations, Los Angeles Chamber Orchestra

Cindy Loeffler
Publicist, The Long Beach Symphony Orchestra

Susanna Bonta
Publicist, The Boston Symphony Orchestra

Kenneth La Fare
Publicist, The New York Philharmonic Orchestra

Jeffrey Reid
Publicist, The Toronto Symphony Orchestra

Juli Hensley
Publicist, San Diego Opera

Ava Jean Mears
Publicist, Houston Grand Opera

Sara Angelucci
Publicist, Canadian Opera Company

Miriam Spiro
Publicist, ICM Artist LTD.

Martin Bernheimer
Music/Dance Critic, Los Angeles Times

Norwell F. Therien, Jr.
Publisher, Prentice Hall

Margaret Antonini
Project Manager, Prentice Hall

My students and teaching assistants at the University of Southern California

ILLUSTRATIONS

FIGURES

PHOTOGRAPHS

1

THE CONCERT

FOR THE FUN OF IT

Half the fun of going to concerts is the anticipation. Buying tickets, getting dressed, and traveling to the hall all help to heighten the enjoyment of the event. You walk into the lobby of the concert hall, gaze at the magnificent staircases, carpets, and hanging art, and you know that something wonderful is about to take place.

After you are escorted to your seat and you look around the hall before the orchestra enters, you begin to feel the tradition of hundreds of years of concert performances. You reach back in time to the great masters of music and become part of it all—because classical music is timeless.

The language of music has no geographical or political boundaries. A 100-piece symphony orchestra may consist of players from a dozen different countries. The soloist may have come from Buenos Aires to perform Tchaikovsky's First Piano Concerto on a Hamburg Steinway in Roy Thompson Hall in Toronto, Ontario. The music still sounds the same.

WHAT TYPES OF CONCERTS ARE THERE?

SYMPHONY ORCHESTRA

Concerts by symphony orchestras have achieved worldwide popularity. Regular concertgoers return year after year to enjoy the symphony orchestra's vast repertoire. Talented and disciplined musicians, who have devoted their lives to perfecting their skills, perform on instruments crafted by the greatest artisans. The rich variety of sounds created by this combination of excellence is a marvel of civilized life and culture.

Is there a difference between a "symphony" orchestra and a "philharmonic" orchestra? No. New York's main orchestra is the New York Philharmonic; Chicago's is the Chicago Symphony. Both are the same size and present similar musical programs. Musically active cities often support more than one major orchestra; one usually is called a philharmonic and the other a symphony orchestra. The designation means nothing.

CHAMBER ORCHESTRA

Originally, chamber orchestras were small groups that performed in the chambers of the 17th- and 18th-century courts and palaces. Mozart and Haydn, for instance, wrote for orchestras of 20–40 performers because

Los Angeles Chamber Orchestra, Christof Perick, Music Director (Courtesy of The Los Angeles Chamber Orchestra/photo by Dana Ross)

palace chambers could accommodate only that number of musicians and a similar size audience. Today, chamber orchestras of 20–60 perform music from all style periods, including contemporary.

The popularity of chamber orchestras has grown rapidly in recent years, especially in cities that already support several large orchestras. Music lovers are discovering that bigger is not necessarily better. If you want to hear chamber orchestra music in the appropriate setting, attend a performance in a small to medium size hall. Much of the great music composed for chamber orchestra loses its original intimacy and clarity in a hall with 3,000 or more seats.

By *clarity* I mean clarity of musical ideas. Like speech, musical ideas make more sense when you can hear them distinctly, which is what composers have in mind. Typical sections of Mozart's and Beethoven's symphonies have short musical ideas played by one instrument, such as an oboe, then imitated by another, such as a flute. Then, the violins pick up the idea in a slightly different manner. You might miss those subtle, charming touches if they are played by a full symphony orchestra in a large hall.

Try an experiment—musicians love to compare performances. Compare a live performance by a large symphony orchestra of a Mozart or Haydn symphony or concerto (recordings do not give the same effect) to a performance of the same work by a chamber orchestra. See if your responses to the two performances differ.

RECITALS

A recital features one or two musicians or a soloist. An artist carefully chooses music to display his or her entire range of musicianship and vocal and instrumental mastery. Figure 1-1 shows the program for soprano Roberta Peters, with piano accompanist Marshall Williamson. Typical of singers, especially opera singers, the program contains songs or *arias* from opera as well as song literature.

Also typical are songs in different languages. Roberta Peters' program includes songs in Italian and German. Some singers might also select works in French, English, or other languages. Because they feel that the original language best expresses the mood of the songs, vocal recitalists as well as opera productions maintain the original language. To assist you in understanding the text, most vocal recital programs provide English translations.

ICM ARTISTS *presents*

Roberta Peters
soprano

Marshall Williamson
piano

MOZART	Voi avete un cor fidele, K. 217
HANDEL	Lascia ch'io piangia, from *Rinaldo*
ROSSINI	Una voce poco fa, from *The Barber of Seville*
R. STRAUSS	*Four Brentano Lieder* An die Nacht Ich wollt' ein Sträusslein binden Säusle, liebe Myrte Amour
VERDI	Caro nome, from *Rigoletto*

intermission

DONIZETTI	Regnava nel silenzio, from *Lucia di Lammermoor* Quel guardo il cavaliere, from *Don Pasquale* O luce di quest'anima, from *Linda di Chamounix*
LEHÁR	Meine Lippen sie küssen so heiß, from *Guiditta* Ich bin verliebt, from *Schön ist die Welt*
SIECZYNSKI	Wien, Wien, nur du allien
LEHÁR	Viljia, from *The Merry Widow*

Figure 1-1   Roberta Peters' Voice Recital Program

Roberta Peters, soprano (Courtesy of ICM Artists, Ltd.)

Encores

In response to the audience's applause after the last piece on the printed program, recitalists usually perform several encores. Encores are usually lighter works and may include unaccompanied pieces and even jazz, musical theater hits, or popular music. These are treated like dessert pieces, meant to thank and please the audience.

In addition to devoted fans, the recital audience usually includes the performer's teacher, family, friends, students, and colleagues—people who really care. Music critics may also be in the audience to review the recital. The whole setting motivates the artist to give the best possible performance.

CHAMBER MUSIC

Chamber music concerts are generally performed by groups of 2–6 musicians, although any combination of 2–20 performers is considered a chamber ensemble. The most common ensembles are string trios and quartets, and brass and woodwind quintets.

Popular as early as the 14th century, chamber music groups performed in the chambers or rooms of the courts and palaces of Europe. Mobility was one reason for this popularity. Players could move easily from chamber to chamber—from the dining room to the study to the outdoors to the balcony to the courtyard—wherever people gathered.

Almost all the great composers of the past three hundred years wrote chamber music: Bach, Handel, Mozart, Haydn, Beethoven, Schumann, Mendelssohn, Brahms, Ravel, Bartok, and Bernstein to name a few. These composers actually wrote more chamber music than their more familiar symphonic masterpieces. Schumann and Brahms, for instance, wrote only four symphonies each, yet each wrote twenty-three works for chamber music ensembles. Beethoven, who wrote only nine symphonies, also wrote eighteen string quartets; five string trios (violin, viola, and cello); two string quintets; ten sonatas for violin and piano; five sonatas for cello and piano; eight trios for violin, cello, and piano; and other chamber works for various combinations of instruments. Since concertgoers mainly attend symphony orchestra performances, relatively few get to know this other side of composers.

Today, most concert music is written for chamber groups. Few composers have a 100-piece symphony orchestra at their disposal, and writing for an orchestra of that size is a more extensive project. Think of the task. It may start with a melody. The composer develops it by adding other melodies, harmony, and rhythm until it finally evolves into a large form. The piece must be orchestrated for 100 instrumentalists playing 25–30 different instruments (many of the 100 musicians play the same parts) and then writing out all the parts. By contrast, a string quartet needs only four parts.

Musicians love the freedom of performing chamber music. In fact, many members of symphony orchestras perform with chamber music groups just for their own pleasure, with or without an audience. Since the small group needs no conductor, each player contributes to the interpretation of the music; each has an important and prominent role.

Great soloists such as Itzhak Perlman, Yo-Yo Ma, Isaac Stern, and Emanuel Ax have stated that their greatest musical enjoyment comes through chamber music performance. Legendary physicist and mathematician Albert Einstein, an amateur violinist, would reschedule meetings with international dignitaries rather than miss a session with his chamber music group.

Tokyo String Quartet, Peter Oundjian (violin), Kikuei Ikeda (violin), Sadao Harada (cello), Kazuhide Isomura (viola) (Courtesy of ICM Artists Ltd.)

CHORAL AND CHURCH MUSIC

Many of the greatest and most moving masterpieces are performed in churches as well as in concert halls:

> *Messiah* by George Frideric Handel
>
> *b minor Mass* by Johann Sebastian Bach
>
> *Requiem* by Wolfgang Amadeus Mozart
>
> *Missa Solemnis* by Ludwig van Beethoven
>
> *Requiem* by Giuseppe Verdi
>
> *War Requiem* by Benjamin Britten

A church or cathedral setting provides the organ to accompany the performers. If you have never heard a great organ, you are missing an extraordinary experience. The organ is the largest and most powerful musical instrument. Rock music groups think they have power when they crank up their amplifiers, but they are merely amplifying distortion. Doing that is like enlarging a photograph until it becomes grainy. An organ produces undistorted sound from assorted pipes as long as thirty-two feet. The rumbling of those sounds can loosen the bricks. That's power!

I directed a brass ensemble for many years at the Riverside Church in New York City where the famous organist Virgil Fox played. During rehearsal, Virgil used to play loud chords on that great organ and laugh when some of the plaster fell from the ceiling. He once joked to me that one day he would find the right combination of sounds to crumble the church. Luckily, he never did!

Hearing music in a great cathedral is like traveling back in a time machine. Surrounded by stained-glass windows, statues, elaborately ornamented pulpits, and magnificent architecture, you can imagine the great Johann Sebastian Bach playing the organ in his church in Leipzig, Germany, accompanying the choir, soloists, and orchestra. (The ornaments, statues, elaborate architecture, and exciting music were the result of a 16th-century version of a Madison Avenue marketing campaign to promote regular churchgoing. It worked.)

Churches and cathedrals have unique acoustics. Music resonates and reverberates in every nook, and the echo can become overwhelming. Earlier composers understood the effect of reverberation and worked it into their compositions. However, I was unaware of its complete effect until I performed with a brass quintet in the huge cathedral in Liverpool, England—the same cathedral for which Paul McCartney composed his *Liverpool Oratorio*.

The program consisted of music from the 16th century to the present. When we started rehearsing, we found we could not perform any of the modern works. In that hall, the reverberation lasted seven seconds. Therefore, dissonances and quick harmonic changes typical of modern music turned into a jumble. We quickly revised our program. Paul McCartney also accommodated the acoustics for the cathedral by writing his oratorio without harmonic dissonances.

Church music varies in length. Many of Bach's almost three hundred cantatas last only 20 minutes because he wrote them for Sunday services in a Lutheran church. Requiems and masses often last up to two hours, while Handel's four-hour *Messiah* is either abridged to run three hours or is presented in two parts: Part One during the Christmas season and Part Two during Easter.

Christmas and Easter offer many excellent church programs. You do not have to be a member of a church or religion to attend these performances.

OPERA

Opera is musical theater, although Richard Wagner preferred to call his operas *music dramas*. Actually, opera is a combination of many theatrical forms: singing, orchestral music, drama, poetry, dance, scenic design, and costume design. Giuseppe Verdi said, "Opera is passion before everything."

The Language of Opera

Europeans have enjoyed opera since its origination in Italy around 1600. Because most of the early operas were written in Italian, it became the most popular language. However, by the late-18th century, librettists used French, German, Russian, English, and other languages.

Coming late to North America, opera has enjoyed tremendous growth in popularity during the last forty years. Since audiences in the United States and Canada use English as their common language, why haven't we translated operas into English for North American performances?

Scene from Act I of Houston Grand Opera production of Gershwin's opera *Porgy and Bess*, featuring Mic Bell as Porgy (Courtesy of the Houston Grand Opera/photo by Jim Caldwell)

As logical as that seems, there are sound arguments against translating opera into English. First, words in opera are difficult to understand regardless of the language. Second, translations can distort the sound of the music.

For example, in the first act of Puccini's opera *La Bohème,* the tenor Rudolfo sings (in Italian) to the soprano Mimi:

"Che gelida manina!"

Here is how that same line translates:

German: "Wie eiskalt sind deine händchen!"

English: "What frozen little hands!"

Translating from the original language takes away some of the flavor—like singing "Home on the Range" in Russian.

Opera has little spoken dialogue; even mundane conversations such as "I think I will go to the kitchen" and "Will you stop that silly chatter, you old goat" are sung. Somehow, Italian makes the chatter sound romantic.

Supertitles

In case you're afraid you won't understand, many opera companies now use electronic English supertitles, translations projected above the proscenium to help the audience follow the story.

PREPARING FOR OPERA

The best way to prepare for opera, regardless of the language, is to read in advance the *libretto* or story. You can find these in the library or as an insert in the record album. Listening to the music from the opera, especially some of the more popular *arias* or songs, also helps.

You can easily obtain at no charge copies of the *Metropolitan Opera Broadcast Guide* at the beginning of each opera season from the Metropolitan Opera, Lincoln Center, New York, NY 10023. The guide contains synopses of the plots scheduled by the Metropolitan Opera for radio and television broadcasts. (See Appendix B for a listing of the Metropolitan Opera Company broadcast stations in your area.)

Once you become an opera fan, you'll have fun following the current "stars," such as Placido Domingo, Luciano Pavarotti, Samuel Ramey, Kiri Te Kanawa, Kathleen Battle, and Marilyn Horne. Their fans are as devoted as those of Bruce Springsteen, Madonna, or Bonnie Raitt.

Be prepared! Most operas last as long as musicals like *Phantom of the Opera* and *Miss Saigon*. Some can last longer. Two outdoor productions in Verona and Rome I recently attended lasted four hours because the stage

crew actually built the sets for each act during the forty-five minute inter-
missions. What an opportunity for an Italian gelato or espresso!

BALLET

Ballet is another wonderful blending of the arts: dance, drama, set design,
costumes, and especially music—the catalyst for the choreography. Many
great masters composed especially for ballet: Beethoven, Berlioz,
Tchaikovsky, Ravel, Stravinsky, Prokofiev, Shostakovich, Copland, and
Bernstein. Ballet orchestras of 40–60 players usually perform in a pit in
front of the stage, like an opera orchestra.

WHAT TYPES OF CONCERT HALLS ARE THERE?

If you investigate, you may be surprised at the number and location of concert halls in your area besides the widely known music centers. Many
receive very little publicity and are in unexpected places such as college
campuses, museums, and auditoriums in corporations and banks.

**Canada's Royal Winnipeg Ballet (Courtesy of Canada's Royal Winnipeg Ballet/photo by
KRG Stills)**

LARGE CONCERT HALLS

Multipurpose concert halls with fifteen hundred to three thousand seats
seem to get the most use. Here are a few examples:

Carnegie Hall, New York City	2,760
Avery Fisher Hall, New York City	2,644
Dorothy Chandler Pavilion, Los Angeles	3,197
Royal Festival Hall, London	3,000
Grosses Festspielhaus, Salzburg	2,177
Grosser Musikvereinssaal, Vienna	1,680

Most of the hall's scheduling revolves around the orchestra, the principal tenant, which may occupy the hall half the time. For example, the
Boston Symphony Orchestra uses Symphony Hall (2,631) as its home base.

**Avery Fisher Hall at the Lincoln Center for the Performing Arts, New York City, home
of the New York Philharmonic Orchestra (Courtesy of Lincoln Center for the
Performing Arts/photo by Norman McGrath)**

The Cleveland Orchestra has Severance Hall (1,890); the Chicago Symphony Orchestra, Orchestra Hall (2,582); Philadelphia Orchestra, Academy of Music (2,983). In some cities, the second resident symphony orchestra and the resident chamber orchestra perform in the same hall as the primary orchestra.

Visiting symphony orchestras and opera and ballet companies are also booked into large concert halls. These groups generally have limited engagements because they must completely take over the hall. They load in sets, lights, and scenery and for ballet, a special wooden floor. Ideally, resident opera and ballet companies have their own theaters.

Jazz artists such as Oscar Peterson, Ella Fitzgerald, Cleo Laine, and Wynton Marsalis need large halls to accommodate their fans. These artists like to perform in the same hall as the symphony orchestra and classical concert artists for another reason: they have achieved equal status. They feel, and I agree with them, that jazz is a serious form of American music and deserves equal status with classical music.

In 1924 George Gershwin made the first breakthrough of jazz to the classical music concert hall. A great controversy arose among concertgoers, concert hall managers, and board members when the noted conductor, Paul Whiteman, commissioned Gershwin to compose *Rhapsody in Blue* for a performance in Aeolian Hall in New York City. Because the work is scored for piano soloist and jazz band, purists considered it unfit for the sacrosanct classical concert hall. After lengthy negotiations, George Gershwin and Paul Whiteman prevailed: the management of Aeolian Hall allowed the new jazz music to have its premiere. George Gershwin himself was the piano soloist with Paul Whiteman conducting.

SMALL AND MEDIUM-SIZED HALLS

Small halls (50–350) seats and medium-sized concert halls (350–1500) are ideal for recitals and chamber music performances. The Stuttgart Liederhalle in Germany has three halls under one roof: the large concert hall (2,000), the medium hall (750), the small hall (350). During the famous annual summer music festival in Mozart's home city of Salzburg, Austria, the "little" (1,323-seat) Festspielhaus hosts concerts of chamber music, solo recitals, and opera.

Some years ago, during a forty-concert tour of Europe with a brass quintet, I performed in some very unusual places: in a tasting room of a winery, on the staircase of a ceramics factory, in the living room of a historic house, in a hotel meeting room, and my favorite, in the original knight's hall in a 14th-century castle. These concerts were in addition to our performances in churches, cathedrals, and traditional concert halls.

Limited audience seating is the main drawback to the small halls, but the advantages are many, particularly the typically better acoustics. Also, it is exciting to be in a hall where Mozart performed, like the Residenz Palace in Salzburg, and to be sitting only a few feet away from performers.

OPERA AND BALLET THEATERS

If you are lucky enough to be in a city with a special hall for opera and ballet, you will see and hear those groups in their best setting. Frequently, the two groups share the same hall because both have similar needs: ideal seating capacity of 1,500; orchestra pit below stage and audience level; a wide proscenium and deep stage to accommodate the scenery; a fly galley to store curtains and sets over the stage; storage space for scenery, props, and costumes for several productions; enough dressing rooms backstage or downstairs.

Examples of famous opera and ballet theaters:

Teatro alla Scala, Milan	2,135
Royal Opera House in Covent Garden, London	2,180
Staatsoper, Hamburg	1,649
Staatsoper, Vienna	1,659
Metropolitan Opera House, New York	3,800

The quality of the hall is so critical with opera that opera buffs travel all over the world to hear performances in the best places. Verdi- and Puccini-lovers attend performances at the famous Teatro alla Scala (La Scala) in Milan to see the works of those composers and other Italian composers performed in a grand manner by some of the world's greatest singers.

Wagner-lovers flock to the Festspielhaus in Bayreuth, Germany. Wagner had this hall specially built for his music-dramas. Situated on a remote hill near Nürnberg, Germany, the hall seats 1,800 on unyielding wood and wicker seats. The huge stage and backstage easily accommodate Wagner's expansive operas. Even the orchestra pit, designed by the composer himself, is unique: its cover opens toward the stage so large orchestras do not overpower the singers.

Russian ballet aficionados prefer the Kirov Theater in St. Petersburg and the Bolshoi Theater in Moscow for the works of Tchaikovsky, Prokofiev, Khatchaturian, and Shostakovich. Enthusiasts of French ballet go to the Paris Opera House for performances of Saint-Saëns, Offenbach, and Delibes.

Try to see an opera or ballet in a great hall. You are in for a memorable experience.

OUTDOOR SHELLS AND SHEDS

Summer is the time for outdoor music. A North American tradition is the town square band shell concert. Summer outdoor concerts are flourishing, and new festival sites develop every year throughout the world.

In the Berkshire Mountains of Massachusetts, the Boston Symphony Orchestra resides every summer at Tanglewood. Located on an incredibly beautiful estate, the shed is unique in that it houses an audience of 6,000 under acoustical conditions that rival the best indoor halls. An additional 6,000 people can enjoy the music sitting casually on the lawn surrounding the shed.

Of the acoustics, Isaac Stern noted, "The Tanglewood Music Shed is

The Tanglewood (Massachusetts) Music Shed, summer home of The Boston Symphony Orchestra (Courtesy of The Boston Symphony Orchestra/photo by Lincoln Russell)

Concert and fireworks at the Hollywood Bowl, summer home of The Los Angeles Philharmonic Orchestra (Courtesy of The Los Angeles Philharmonic Orchestra)

one of the most fantastically successful efforts to create brilliant, ringing sound with wonderful definition, despite the enormous size of the hall. It is particularly successful in providing an equal sound value wherever one sits. On stage there is a wonderfully live quality, and yet complete clarity for balancing with the orchestra."

An elegant picnic before the performance has become a Tanglewood tradition. Concertgoers bring lawn chairs or blankets, fine wine and food, even candles for illumination. And afterward, they listen to great music under a display of brilliant stars. Is there a finer way to spend an evening?

Another splendid outdoor summer music festival site is the Hollywood Bowl in Los Angeles, the summer home of the Los Angeles Philharmonic. A full house is 17,680. The audience sits under a starlit sky, with evening temperatures in the low 70s.

The Bowl is a favorite of Californians as well as visitors who realize that their chances are excellent of spotting some celebrities. Before the concert, picnickers are everywhere—in special picnic areas, in the seats, along the walkways. Box seat holders can rent portable tables, and picnic dinners are available for purchase. Some arrange for special caterers to deliver everything to the box, prepare and serve the meal, and then carry everything away before the concert starts. What else would you expect in Hollywood!

One night I had guests at my home during a Bowl concert—the annual "Tchaikovsky Spectacular"—which includes, among other works, the *1812 Overture*. Cannons, rifle fire, bells, and fireworks were among the added attractions. We could hear the music as we sat in the living room. Suddenly, clouds of smoke from the cannons and rifles drew us outdoors. Another year at a similar performance of the *1812 Overture*, the breeze swept the smoke into the shell, engulfing the musicians who never missed a beat while they continued performing. Oh, the life of a performing musician!

Other famous summer outdoor music festival sites are Central Park Mall in New York, Wolf Trap Farm in Virginia, the Aspen Music Festival in Colorado, and the Blossom Music Festival in Ohio. Consult your newspapers for the outdoor concert sites near you. If you are traveling in the United States or Europe, automobile club and tourist information bureaus have directories of festivals along your route, and they often provide discount ticket coupons. Look for them—they may be the highlight of your next trip.

The New York Philharmonic Orchestra performing in Central Park (Courtesy of The New York Philharmonic Orchestra)

How Can I Find Out About Concerts and Tickets?

NEWSPAPERS

Concert advertisements include phone numbers for ticket purchases, credit card information, box office location and hours, and the time, location, program, and artists for the concert. Many ads also mention if there is wheelchair access. If you have questions, call the box office directly, not the ticket agency or "charge" line. Box office personnel are knowledgeable and helpful.

Relying solely on newspapers for ticket information, you may not get the best seats, and sometimes the house may have already been sold out. Some alternatives follow.

MAILING LISTS

For earliest notification about concerts, put your name on the mailing list for the hall or for events you are interested in. Call or write a short note to the concert hall or series management. You will be placed on their mailing list for several years. (If you move, let them know.)

Once you are on the list, you will receive advance ticket information—before it is advertised in the newspapers. You can order early by mail and get the ticket prices and seats you want. There will be no extra service charge, and you can save gas, time, and possible disappointment.

Season Subscriptions

Subscribers have the best seats. Once you determine the series of programs and seats you prefer—I will discuss this shortly—you can reserve them for the entire season. Further advantages begin in the second year. As a season subscriber, you will be notified of the coming concert season before those who are on the general mailing lists. Also, since most concert series allow you to retain the same seats from year to year or to improve them, you'll have the seats you want. A simple reorder form will come in the mail. Send it back with your payment, and you will have your tickets for the entire season. You may even have the advantage of special subscribers' discounts.

When you have a season subscription, you may notice the same people around you at nearly every concert. They too are subscribers. Your chances are good of developing interesting acquaintanceships through repeated contacts.

PURCHASING TICKETS

Box Office

Obviously, you can always purchase tickets at the box office if a performance isn't sold out. If you are not familiar with a particular hall, plan to get to the box office as far in advance as possible. If tickets are available, you can purchase them immediately before the concert. Just walk up to the box office window and get them, like going to a movie. Of course, you run the risk of not getting your first choice of seat or of having to pay more than you planned because the less expensive seats are sold.

Ticket Outlets

Many concert organizations use computerized ticket outlets or charge lines where you can order tickets by phone and have them mailed to your home, or pick them up in person. Using these services may be more convenient than traveling to the box office, even though you may pay a nominal charge for the transaction. In some cases, ticket outlets have essentially the same tickets as the box office because they are hooked up to a central computer. However, they can't guarantee you particular seats. In other cases, the concert hall or management designates particular blocks of seats for the outlets.

Suggestion: Whether you buy your tickets by phone from the box office or from a ticket outlet, have the tickets mailed to you, if possible. Then you won't have to stand in the "will-call" line just before the performance.

Student Rush Tickets

Students may have a considerable advantage in going to the box office within an hour of the concert. Most orchestra concerts, operas, and ballets offer reduced prices for "student rush." For as little as $5 or $10 you can get seats originally priced several times that amount. You must show current student identification, which usually entitles you to buy only one ticket.

Senior Citizen Tickets

Senior citizens (you may also be asked to show identification) sometimes have opportunities to buy tickets at reduced prices. Ads and brochures will specifically mention these offers and the age considered "senior." To be sure you qualify, call the box office.

Group Discounts

Check ads and brochures for a special group sales phone number. Your social, professional, or religious organization may be entitled to special rates if you buy a block of tickets. You can even organize a group of friends or relatives to get these rates, if they are available.

Personnel and Employee Relations Discounts

Businesses, especially large corporations, are often given a block of tickets or employee discount coupons by concert organizations. It can't hurt to check with your company's Human Resources Department or Employee Benefits Office. You might save $5 to $10 or more per ticket.

A REMINDER TO SEASON TICKET HOLDERS: If you cannot attend a performance, please call the box office to let them know. This notification releases your tickets for the student rush ticket pool. You don't have to mail your tickets back; the box office usually accepts your phone call as notice up to the start of the performance. Even though you will not receive a refund, you'll be doing a great service for students who might otherwise be

John Williams conducts The Boston Pops Orchestra performance at Symphony Hall, Boston (Courtesy of The Boston Pops Orchestra/photo by Miro Vinton, IV)

turned away from a performance that has vacant seats. Performers hate to see those empty seats, and you will have the satisfaction of knowing that an eager student took your place.

WHERE SHOULD I SIT AT CONCERTS?

Where you sit can be as important to your enjoyment as the program itself. To find the seat that suits you and your wallet, get to know the concert hall. Figure 1-2 shows a typical concert hall layout and rates each location by number.

Seating Plans

Seating plans are available through many sources. The box office has them posted. If not, just ask for a copy. If you live in a large city, check your bookstores for commercially published seating plans for all the theaters and concert halls. Some local classical music stations make seating plans available through the mail. You can always get help from your librarian. Also, check the front of your telephone book.

Advice From the Box Office

Box office personnel are helpful in recommending places to sit. If you ask, they will even advise you on the best seats for each price ticket.

Try Various Locations

Until you find your preferred location in a particular concert hall, you might try purchasing seats for different concerts in various locations, such as the balcony, loge, and orchestra.

THE BEST SEATS IN THE HOUSE

Every concert hall has different acoustical engineering, but regular concert-goers generally have several favorite locations in any hall, usually the center of the orchestra and the first few rows of the next level (called mezzanine, parquet terrace, loge, or even founders circle). These seats are usually the most expensive, though price alone is not the only criterion for seat selection. In many halls, the best seats for sound may be in the upper balconies and cost less than orchestra section seats. (Refer to Figure 1-2 for ratings of locations in a typical hall.)

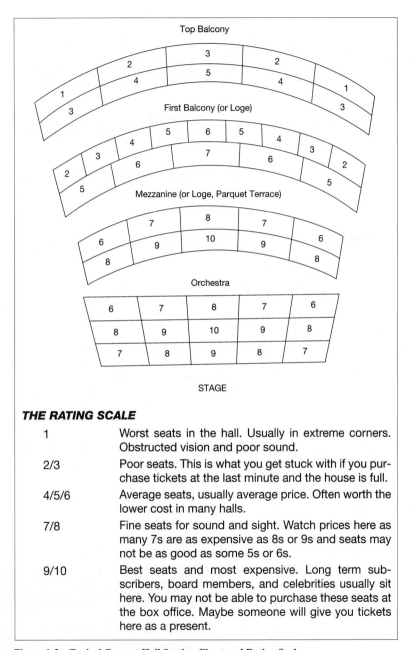

THE RATING SCALE

1	Worst seats in the hall. Usually in extreme corners. Obstructed vision and poor sound.
2/3	Poor seats. This is what you get stuck with if you purchase tickets at the last minute and the house is full.
4/5/6	Average seats, usually average price. Often worth the lower cost in many halls.
7/8	Fine seats for sound and sight. Watch prices here as many 7s are as expensive as 8s or 9s and seats may not be as good as some 5s or 6s.
9/10	Best seats and most expensive. Long term subscribers, board members, and celebrities usually sit here. You may not be able to purchase these seats at the box office. Maybe someone will give you tickets here as a present.

Figure 1-2   Typical Concert Hall Seating Chart and Rating Scale

OTHER TIPS ON SEATING

If the expression on a soloist's face is important to you, by all means sit in the orchestra section close to the stage. However, you will sacrifice some views of the musicians at the rear of the stage, and the sound and view are usually better from farther back in the orchestra section or on the next level. Also try to avoid sitting far back under a balcony or overhang, which may block the sound and create an echo. And if you enjoy watching a pianist's hands, sit on the left side of the hall.

DISABLED PARKING AND SEATING

For patrons with limited mobility, most concert halls have special parking, wheelchair ramps, lifts, convenient seating, and well-designed restrooms. Easily accessed areas, usually at the side or in the rear of the orchestra section, are reserved for wheelchairs. Many concert associations will arrange adjacent or nearby seating for those who assist with wheelchairs.

SUGGESTIONS FOR YOUR FIRST CONCERT

POPS ORCHESTRA

If you haven't been to many classical music concerts, consider starting with a "pops" orchestra concert. The program will have the broad appeal of lighter classics and even popular commercial music—thus, the designation "pops." Classical music definitely has its clever, lighter, and fun-loving side.

The Boston Pops might play ballet music such as excerpts from *Rodeo* by Aaron Copland, or the "Sabre Dance" from the *Gayne* Ballet by Aram Khachaturian. The Pops also programs excerpts from modern musical theater or film hits such as *Phantom of the Opera* by Andrew Lloyd Webber, or John Williams' *Star Wars* and *JFK*. To add variety, the concert may also feature a well-known soloist or jazz artist.

Pops concerts make a great evening's entertainment even for the serious music lover. Notice the variety of styles of music in the program of a recent concert by the Boston Pops Orchestra in Figure 1-3.

SUMMER FESTIVAL ORCHESTRAS

If the area where you live has a summer music festival, try to take advantage of it. The music is usually lively and especially appealing to outdoor audiences. Read the publicity and choose one you'd like. The pleasant set-

BOSTON POPS ORCHESTRA
JOHN WILLIAMS, conductor

Olympic Fanfare	Williams
Appalachian Morning	Hally-P. Williams
Theme from *JFK* Timothy Morrison, solo trumpet	Williams
On the Trail, from *Grand Canyon* Suite	Grofe

INTERMISSION

Galop from *Moscow Cheremushky*	Shostakovich
Concertino for marimba and orchestra Vigorous Calm Lively J. William Hudgins, marimba	Creston
Dance finale from Estancia	Ginastera

INTERMISSION

Lover, from *Love Me Tonight*	Rodgers-Morley
Selections from *Beauty and the Beast* Prologue—Belle—Gaston—Something There— Be Our Guest—Beauty and the Beast	Menken-Ramin
Unforgettable Bob Winter, piano	Gordon-Morley
Excerpts from *Far and Away* County Galway, June 1982—The Fighting Donnellys— Joseph and Shannon—Blowing off Steam (The Fight)— Finale Jerry O'Sullivan, uilleann pipes	Williams

Figure 1-3   Boston Pops Orchestra Concert Program

ting, along with the beverages and snacks, makes for a very delightful concert. Perfect for a date!

SYMPHONY ORCHESTRAS

If no pops or summer festival concerts are available, my next suggestion would be a regular season concert by your city's resident symphony orchestra or by the orchestra of your local university. Just watch for their announced programs and pick a good first concert for you. Figure 1-4 shows an example of an interesting program presented by The Philadelphia Orchestra conducted by Riccardo Muti.

WHAT KIND OF MUSICAL PROGRAM SHOULD I LOOK FOR?

For many years, listeners of one of the classical radio stations in Los Angeles voted on their "Top 40" favorites. These listeners are seasoned concertgoers, and the station published their choices, which are typical of national audiences. A few pieces (which I have noted) are for chorus and orchestra, ballet, opera, piano, organ or other solo instruments; the rest are orchestral pieces.

Top 40 Classical Favorites

Rank	Composer	Title
1	Beethoven	Symphony No. 9 in d minor (*Choral*)
2	Ravel	*Bolero*
3	Beethoven	Symphony No. 5 in c minor
4	Beethoven	Symphony No. 6 in F Major (*Pastoral*)
5	Vivaldi	*The Four Seasons*
6	Pachelbel	Canon in D Major
7	Handel	*Messiah* (oratorio—vocal soloists with choir and orchestra)
8	Beethoven	Symphony No. 7 in A Major
9	Verdi	*Requiem* (vocal soloists with choir and orchestra)
10	Rachmaninoff	Piano Concerto No. 2 in c minor
11	Tchaikovsky	*1812 Overture*
12	Bach	*Brandenburg* Concertos (all six)
13	Tchaikovsky	Suite from *The Nutcracker* (ballet)
14	Tchaikovsky	Piano Concerto No. 1 in b-flat minor

THE PHILADELPHIA ORCHESTRA

RICCARDO MUTI, *music director*

Riccardo Muti, *conductor*
Murray W. Panitz, *flute*
Richard Woodhams, *oboe*
Anthony M. Gigliotti, *clarinet*
Nolan Miller, *horn*
Bernard Garfield, *bassoon*

Concerto for Wind Quintet and Orchestra (1960)   Etler

> **I. Maestoso–Allegro moderato–Vivace**
> **II. Lento**
> **III. Allegro energico**

Suite from *The Firebird* (1919 version)   Stravinsky

> **I. Introduction–The Firebird and Its Dance**
> **II. The Princesses' Round Dance**
> **III. Infernal Dance of King Kashchei**
> **IV. Berceuse**
> **V. Finale**

intermission

Symphony No. 5 in c minor Opus 67   Beethoven

> **I. Allegro con brio**
> **II. Andante con moto**
> **III. Scherzo: Allegro**
> **IV. Allegro**

Figure 1-4   Philadelphia Orchestra Concert Program

15	Bach	Toccata and Fugue in d minor (organ solo)
16	Beethoven	Piano Concerto No. 5 in E-Flat Major (*Emperor*)
17	Tchaikovsky	*Swan Lake* (ballet)
18	Beethoven	Symphony No. 3 in E-Flat Major (*Eroica*)
19	Debussy	*Clair de lune* (piano solo)
20	Gershwin	*Rhapsody in Blue*
21	Brahms	Symphony No. 4 in e minor
22	Rimsky-Korsakov	*Scheherazade*
23	Chopin	Polonaise in A-Flat Major (piano solo)
24	Dvŏrák	Symphony No. 9 in e minor (*New World*)
25	Mozart	Symphony No. 40 in g minor
26	Stravinsky	*The Rite of Spring* (*Le Sacre du printemps*)
27	Beethoven	*Moonlight* Sonata (piano solo)
28	Brahms	Symphony No. 1 in c minor
29	Grieg	Piano Concerto in a minor
30	Mozart	*Eine kleine Nachtmusik*
31	Beethoven	Violin Concerto in D Major
32	Bach	Mass in b minor (vocal soloists with choir and orchestra)
33	Mahler	Symphony No. 1 in D Major (*Titan*)
34	Tchaikovsky	Symphony No. 5 in e minor
35	Mozart	*Requiem* (vocal soloists with choir and orchestra)
36	Berlioz	*Symphonie fantastique*
37	Mussorgsky	*Pictures at an Exhibition*
38	Rachmaninoff	*Rhapsody on a Theme of Paganini*
39	Mozart	Piano Concerto No. 21 in C Major
40	Puccini	*La Bohème* (opera)

ORCHESTRAL MUSIC

As an indication of the popularity of orchestral music, thirty-one of the "Top 40 Classical Favorites" are works for orchestra. You can use the list as a reference point for choosing concerts and for building your personal record collection (see Appendix A). Also, you will often hear the following 100 compositions in orchestra concerts.

Composer	*Title*
Bach	Orchestral Suites (all four)
Bartók	*Concerto for Orchestra*

Riccardo Muti, Music Director of The Philadelphia Orchestra acknowledging the audience's applause (Courtesy of The Philadelphia Orchestra/photo by Steve J. Sherman)

Beethoven	Symphony No. 2 in D Major
Beethoven	Piano Concertos (Nos. 1–4)
Berlioz	*Harold in Italy*
Berlioz	*Roman Carnival Overture*
Bernstein	Suite from *West Side Story*
Bizet	*Carmen* Suite
Bizet	Symphony No. 1 in C Major
Bloch	*Schelomo*—Rhapsody for Cello and Orchestra
Borodin	*In the Steppes of Central Asia*
Borodin	Polovtzian Dances from *Prince Igor*
Brahms	*Academic Festival Overture*
Brahms	*Alto Rhapsody*
Brahms	Symphony No. 2 in D Major
Brahms	Symphony No. 3 in F Major
Brahms	Piano Concerto No. 1 in d minor
Brahms	Violin Concerto in D Major
Bruch	Violin Concerto No. 1 in g minor
Chopin	Piano Concerto No. 1 in e minor
Copland	*Appalachian Spring*
Copland	*El salón México*

Copland	Suite from *Billy the Kid*
Copland	Suite from *Rodeo*
Debussy	*Afternoon of a Faun*
Debussy	*Iberia*
Debussy	*Images*
Debussy	*La Mer*
Dvořák	*Carnival Overture*
Dvořák	*Slavonic Dances*
Dvořák	Cello Concerto in b minor
Elgar	*Enigma Variations*
Falla	*Nights in the Gardens of Spain*
Falla	Suite from *The Three-Cornered Hat*
Gershwin	*An American in Paris*
Gershwin	Piano Concerto in F Major
Grofé	*Grand Canyon Suite*
Handel	*The Royal Fireworks Music*
Handel	*The Water Music*
Haydn	Symphony No. 88 in G Major
Haydn	Symphony No. 94 in G Major (*Surprise*)
Haydn	Symphony No. 101 in D Major (*Clock*)
Haydn	Trumpet Concerto in E-Flat Major
Hindemith	*Mathis der Maler*
Holst	*The Planets*
Ibert	*Ports of Call*
Ives	*Symphony: Holidays*
Ives	Symphony No. 2
Kodály	*Háry János Suite*
Lalo	*Symphonie espagnole*
Liszt	*Les Preludes*
Liszt	Piano Concerto No. 1 in E-Flat Major
Mahler	*Songs of a Wayfarer*
Mahler	Symphony No. 4 in G Major
Mendelssohn	*Hebrides Overture (Fingal's Cave)*
Mendelssohn	Overture to *A Midsummer Night's Dream*
Mendelssohn	Symphony No. 4 in A Major (*Italian*)
Mendelssohn	Violin Concerto in e minor
Mozart	Symphony No. 35 in D Major (*Haffner*)
Mozart	Symphony No. 41 in C Major (*Jupiter*)
Mussorgsky	*A Night on Bald Mountain*
Prokofiev	*Lieutenant Kijé Suite*

Prokofiev	Symphony No. 1 in D Major (*Classical*)
Prokofiev	Symphony No. 5
Prokofiev	Piano Concerto No. 2 in g minor
Ravel	*Rhapsodie espagnole*
Ravel	Suite from *Daphnis and Chloé*
Ravel	Piano Concerto in G Major
Respighi	*Fountains of Rome*
Respighi	*Pines of Rome*
Respighi	*The Birds*
Rimsky-Korsakov	*Capriccio espagnol*
Rimsky-Korsakov	*Russian Easter Overture*
Rossini	Overture to *The Barber of Seville*
Rossini	Overture to *The Thieving Magpie*
Rossini	Overture to *William Tell*
Schubert	Symphony No. 8 in b minor (*Unfinished*)
Schubert	Symphony No. 9 in C Major (*Great*)
Schumann	Symphony No. 1 in B-Flat Major (*Spring*)
Schumann	Piano Concerto in a minor
Shostakovich	Symphony No. 5
Smetana	*The Moldau*
Strauss, R.	*Death and Transfiguration* *(Tod und Verklärung)*
Strauss, R.	*Don Juan*
Strauss, R.	*Ein Heldenleben (A Hero's Life)*
Strauss, R.	*Till Eulenspiegel's Merry Pranks* *(Till Eulenspiegels lustige Streiche)*
Stravinsky	*Firebird* Suite
Stravinsky	*Petrushka* Suite
Tchaikovsky	*Capriccio Italien*
Tchaikovsky	*Romeo and Juliet Overture-Fantasia*
Tchaikovsky	Symphony No. 4 in f minor
Tchaikovsky	Symphony No. 6 in b minor (*Pathétique*)
Tchaikovsky	Violin Concerto in D Major
Vaughan Williams	*Fantasia on a Theme of Thomas Tallis*
Vaughan Williams	Symphony No. 2 (*London*)
Wagner	Overture to *Die Meistersinger von Nürnberg*
Wagner	Overture to *The Flying Dutchman*
Wagner	Prelude to *Tristan and Isolde*
Weber	Overture to *Der Freischütz*
Weber	Overture to *Oberon*

Canada's Royal Winnipeg Ballet performing *Grand Pas Espagñol* (Courtesy of Canada's Royal Winnipeg Ballet/photo by KRG Stills)

BALLET

Going to the ballet as one of your first concert experiences can be thrilling. The dance music is lively and rhythmic. The choreography usually depicts a story which helps you relate to the music. And there's little to compare with the eye appeal of the dancing, theater, sets, and costumes—very colorful and theatrical. The "Top 40" hits include a few ballet works:

Composer	*Title*
Stravinsky	*The Rite of Spring (Le Sacre du printemps)*
Tchaikovsky	*The Nutcracker*
Tchaikovsky	*Swan Lake*

Besides the music originally intended for ballet, great composers have written music that lends itself to the dance. What a challenge for a choreographer—to create a work based on a musical masterpiece! Although Bach, Handel, Mozart, and others might not have conceived their compositions for choreography, many great ballets have been designed for their music.

Here are some other suggestions for your first ballet performance, including all categories of ballet music:

Composer	Title	Choreographer
Bach	Concerto Barocco	Balanchine
Bizet	Symphony in C	Balanchine
Chausson	Lilac Garden	Tudor
Copland	Appalachian Spring	Graham
Copland	Billy the Kid	DeMille
Copland	Rodeo	DeMille
Debussy	Afternoon of a Faun	Robbins
Field, John	Pas des Deesses	Joffrey
Gould	Fall River Legend	DeMille
Mahler	Round of Angels	Arpino
Mendelssohn	Midsummer Night's Dream	Balanchine
Mozart	Sinfonia Concertante	McMillan
Prokofiev	Romeo and Juliet	McMillan
Tchaikovsky	Theme and Variation	Balanchine
Tchaikovsky	Serenade	Balanchine

CHURCH AND CHORAL MUSIC

Let's start with three works that were listed on the "Top 40" hits:

Composer	Title
Bach	Mass in b minor
Handel	Messiah
Verdi	Requiem

These three are excellent choices for first performances of church and choral music. Most of the music in this category will be long and, of course, fairly serious. But the combined forces of vocal soloists, large chorus, and orchestra performing in a beautiful hall or church should offer an excellent musical experience.

Here is an additional list of suggested works I think you will enjoy:

Composer	Title
Bach	Cantatas Nos. 4, 51, 140
Bach	Christmas Oratorio
Bach	Magnificat in D

Beethoven	*Missa Solemnis*
Bernstein	*Mass* (theater piece)
Brahms	*A German Requiem*
Britten	*A Ceremony of Carols*
Britten	*War Requiem*
Bruckner	Mass in e minor
Handel	*Judas Maccabeus*
Handel	*Solomon*
Haydn	*The Creation*
Haydn	*The Seasons*
Kodály	*Te Deum*
Schubert	Mass in G Major
Stravinsky	*Mass*
Stravinsky	*Symphony of Psalms*

OPERA

One opera made the "Top 40" list: Puccini's *La Bohéme*—an excellent choice for newcomers to opera. Here are a few more suggestions (in order of my preference):

Composer	Title	
Gershwin	*Porgy and Bess*	
Bizet	*Carmen*	
Menotti	*Amahl and the Night Visitors*	
Weill	*Threepenny Opera*	
Puccini	*Madame Butterfly*	
Verdi	*Rigoletto*	
Gounod	*Faust*	
Mozart	*The Magic Flute*	
Verdi	*Otello*	
Mozart	*Don Giovanni*	
Verdi	*La Traviata*	
Mascagni	*Cavalleria Rusticana*	(usually on the same
Leoncavallo	*Pagliacci*	program)
Verdi	*Aida*	
Offenbach	*Tales of Hoffmann*	
Puccini	*Tosca*	
Puccini	*Turandot*	
Mussorgsky	*Boris Godunov*	

Strauss, J.	*Die Fledermaus*
Strauss, R.	*Salome*
Wagner	*Die Meistersinger von Nürnberg*
Smetana	*The Bartered Bride*
Verdi	*Falstaff*
Britten	*Peter Grimes*
Moore	*The Ballad of Baby Doe*
Mozart	*Abduction from the Seraglio*
Mozart	*The Marriage of Figaro*
Verdi	*Il trovatore*
Bucci	*Sweet Molly from Pike*

HOW SHOULD I DRESS FOR CONCERTS?

Once upon a time, when a concert was more of a social event where people went to be seen and to watch others, it was tradition to get dressed up in one's "Sunday best." Since the 1970s, however, audiences have been dressing more casually, attending concerts to hear the music rather than to display their finery. But don't be surprised if you see tradition-bound concertgoers wearing tuxedos and formal gowns.

What you wear is up to you. Less formal dress may be the trend, but it's a matter of appropriateness. You should consider your choice of attire as a symbol of respect for the performers.

OPENING NIGHT

Opening night of the symphony, opera, or ballet season is a special event. Men in black ties and tuxedos or women in evening gowns are common sights, but that formality is not required. What you would wear to a house of worship or to an afternoon wedding will fit in nicely.

OUTDOOR SUMMER CONCERTS AND POPS CONCERTS

These concerts are the least formal, so the dress is the most casual. Wear something comfortable, especially if you are sitting on the lawn. Again, there are limits. Jeans and sports clothes are acceptable, but some concert managers will not admit you in beach clothes.

Suggestion: Overdressing can be just as inappropriate as underdressing. It is probably better to dress a bit conservatively until you learn how others dress for a particular concert.

HOW CAN I PREPARE FOR A CONCERT?

BECOME ACQUAINTED WITH THE MUSIC

Listen to recordings of the music that will be on the program. Most concert music is available on compact discs, tape cassettes, and records. Besides preparing for the concert, you can build your personal classical music record collection. (For a recommended basic record collection, see Appendix A.)

Before going to the concert and while you are listening to the recordings, read Chapters 3 and 4. You'll find detailed instructions to guide your listening.

Play music whenever you can—on your pocket cassette player, while exercising, cooking, cleaning, or puttering around your home. Get to know as much music as you can. As with most things in life—friends, sports, food, hobbies, and art—we like what we know best.

Also, pre-set your radio to your classical music station. Appendix B lists North American radio stations featuring classical music. While maneuvering in bumper-to-bumper traffic, you can relax and use the time profitably by listening to great music. If your local classical music station takes requests, you might ask for a particular piece to help you prepare for your next concert.

Municipal and university libraries are also excellent resources for recordings. Most have facilities where you can sit and listen for hours.

GET TO KNOW THE COMPOSER, ARTISTS, AND BACKGROUND OF THE MUSIC

Composers' biographies are fascinating. Many of the greatest geniuses made human errors in their everyday lives. Their stories are very moving. A record jacket is one of the most easily obtainable sources for information about a composer, conductor, the performers, and the music. Record companies gear the information mostly for non-musicians and avoid technical language. It's a good place to start.

Appendix D lists additional reading and information on sources for composers, specific compositions, style periods, and terminology.

A music dictionary is a handy item. I recommend the inexpensive paperback *Harvard Brief Dictionary of Music* by Ralph Daniel and Willie Apel. It has useful information about musical terms, instruments, and notation.

For a detailed history of the development of concert music, you may want to own the excellent book by Donald Grout, *A History of Western Music.* For an overview of the major musical styles, important composers, and related arts, I recommend my own book, *Listening to Music,* which comes with a coordinated set of cassette tapes and compact discs.

Appendix D also lists magazines specializing in classical music and the concert world. Both *Ovation* and *Musical America,* for example, contain current articles on performers and their travels, composers, recordings, and other related fields. To help you build your personal record collection, magazines such as *High Fidelity, CD Review,* and *Stereo Review* contain discussions and reviews of the latest recording releases. (See Appendix A for a suggested basic record collection.)

For opera devotees, a subscription to the Metropolitan Opera's publication, *Opera News,* could be an excellent resource about opera recordings and Metropolitan Opera performances and national broadcasts (Appendix B: Texaco Metropolitan Opera Radio Broadcasts was provided by *Opera News*).

MAY I RECORD THE CONCERT?

Without express permission of the concert management, you may not bring a recorder into the hall. First of all, recording at the concert annoys nearby listeners. Also, most organizations and performers professionally record their artistry. Therefore, "pirate" recordings are a form of plagiarism. Performers and composers rely on sales of their efforts. Despite their remarkable talents, live performances by classical artists command far lower compensation than pop and rock artists, not to mention fees exacted by sports figures.

ARE THERE OTHER ITEMS I SHOULD NOT BRING INTO THE CONCERT HALL?

Please do not bring any pagers (beepers) and portable phones into the concert hall. Murphy must have written some "law" about those items because they tend to ring or buzz during the quietest passages. Deactivate your watch if you have set the alarm or an hourly beep. Leave your camera at home. Flash photography during a concert is prohibited. Not only is it disrespectful to performers, but it is also a distraction.

At indoor concerts, food and drinks are not allowed. However, at outdoor programs, food and drink are not only allowed, but they are a part of the concert ambiance. If you have questions about what you can bring to a concert, check with the box office.

WHAT IS IN THE PRINTED PROGRAM?

When you are seated, you will usually receive a free copy of the printed concert program. Occasionally, there may be a modest charge, but you do not have to buy the program. Actually, most concert organizations prefer to provide their programs at no charge, but with dwindling government support for the arts, extra charges have become a necessity.

Concert programs contain a variety of useful information in addition to the usual who, what, where, and when. Often, detailed program notes will describe the music and provide historical background for the pieces. These notes will be similar to those on record jackets, though more extensive.

Concert Overview

Usually, one page of the program contains an overview of the concert. Most listeners follow the program's progress on this page. Even in a multipage program there will be an overview page. Let's look at a typical overview page for a concert by the London Symphony Orchestra and discuss some of the program items (Figure 1-5).

Key or Tonality

Examining the London Symphony program, notice that the symphonies and the concertos also specify the main key or tonality of the work—Beethoven's Symphony in c minor, for example (Figure 1-5).

Catalog Designations

The Op. and K. markings are catalog designations of the composer's works, usually in chronological order. The designation "Op. 36" after the title of Tchaikovsky's *Symphony No. 4* refers to the order among all his compositions in which he wrote that work—*opus,* meaning "work" in Latin. In this case, the *Symphony No. 4* was approximately his thirty-sixth composition.

In place of opus numbers, some composers' works bear another designation, usually assigned by the person who catalogued the music. Notice that Mozart's *Clarinet Concerto* carries the designation "K. 622." Mozart was so prolific and generally rushed for time that he didn't keep his works in a very tidy order. More than 50 years after Mozart's death, Ludwig von Köchel (1800–77) catalogued the vast collection of his works. Köchel paid homage to Mozart by arranging his works in a generally precise sequence.

LONDON SYMPHONY ORCHESTRA
MICHAEL TILSON THOMAS, Conductor

LUDWIG VAN BEETHOVEN

Symphony No. 5 in c minor, Op. 68 (1808)

Allegro con brio
Andante con moto
Allegro, *leading into*
Allegro

WOLFGANG AMADEUS MOZART

Concerto in A Major for Clarinet and Orchestra, K. 622 (1791)

Allegro
Adagio
Rondo: Allegro

Franz Hoeprich, Clarinet Soloist

Intermission

PETER ILYICH TCHAIKOVSKY

Symphony No. 4 in f minor, Op. 36 (1877)

Andante sostenuto; Moderato con anima
Andantino in modo di canzona
Scherzo: Pizzicato ostinato
Allegro con fuoco

GEORGE GERSHWIN

Concerto in F Major for Piano and Orchestra

Allegro
Andante con moto
Allegro con brio

Michael Tilson Thomas, Piano Soloist/Conductor

Figure 1-5   London Symphony Orchestra Concert Program

The following table lists some of the most commonly used designations:

Common Music Catalog Designations

Composer	Designation	Cataloguer
Bach, J. S.	BWV	Wolfgang Schmieder: Thematisch-systematisches Verzeichnis der musikalischen Werke von Johann Sebastian Bach
Haydn	H. or Hob.	A. van Hoboken
Mozart	K.	Ludwig von Köchel
Schubert	D.	O. E. Deutsch
Vivaldi	R. or P.	Peter Ryom

Movements and Tempo Indications

Referring again to the London Symphony program, notice the Italian terms after the title, each on a separate line. These terms are the movements, tempo, and style indications the composer placed on the music. Listeners use the terms to keep track of the different movements. Since the first term usually refers to the speed or tempo of the music, we can easily discover which movement we are listening to. The Italian terms after the first tempo term are modifiers or style of the tempo. For example, in Gershwin's Piano Concerto in F, the first movement is marked Allegro (lively or fast); the second, Andante con moto (slow to moderate tempo with movement); the last, Allegro con brio (lively with spirit). Studying these terms will help you become a very knowledgeable listener. To assist you with the Italian terminology, here is a chart of the most common tempo terms and the descriptions used with them. (See Glossary for additional terms.)

Common Tempo Terms and Descriptions

(from slow to fast)	
grave	extremely slow and solemnly
largo	very slow, broadly
lento	slow
adagio	slow, leisurely
andante	slow to moderate walking pace
moderato	moderate
allegretto	moderately fast
allegro	fast, lively
vivace	very fast
presto	very fast
prestissimo	as fast as possible

Descriptions Often Used with Tempos

agitato	agitated
animato	animated
cantabile	singing style
con brio	with spirit
con fuoco	with fire
con moto	with movement
e or ed.	and
espressivo	expressively
grazioso	gracefully
ma	but
ma non troppo	but not too much

WHAT CONCERT TRADITIONS
SHOULD I KNOW ABOUT?

Like every activity that brings people together, music has its own formalities and traditions. Church music programs go back thousands of years; public concerts go back hundreds. Naturally, that long a time span produces many interesting customs—all part of the enjoyment. The rich heritage of music traditions has been honored by kings and queens, heads of state, noblemen and peasants, artists, thinkers, and of course, music lovers.

What follows will give you an idea of traditions and rituals to expect at concerts. Remember, these are not laws or rules, and nobody follows them to the letter.

SYMPHONY ORCHESTRA CONCERT PROCEDURE

HOW DOES THE ORCHESTRA ENTER THE STAGE?   Members of a university orchestra might be instructed to enter at the same time. Professional musicians seem to stroll randomly to their seats. In fact, most orchestra musicians resist regimentation; they are already committed and disciplined. The orchestra comprises individual artists who have consented to perform together, with the aid of the conductor. That, of course, is the orchestral musician's point of view. The conductor and management may have another.

As for making their entrance, wind players and percussionists tend to go to their seats early—about ten minutes before the concert starts. They need to set out a lot of equipment—reeds for the woodwinds; mallets, cym-

Seiji Ozawa, Music Director of The Boston Symphony Orchestra (Courtesy of The Boston Symphony Orchestra/photo by Steve J. Sherman)

bals, and so forth, for the percussion; and mutes for the brass instruments. Brass players take their seats long before the concert begins to get their instruments accustomed to the temperature of the stage.

HOW DO THE PLAYERS WARM UP?   Warming up is an important part of a musician's performance. Like an athlete, a musician must limber up very delicate muscles. Surgeons and medical researchers who have studied the neural-muscular system claim that performing music on an instrument is the most highly skilled use of the whole system. Musicians must move fingers and limbs in split-second accuracy, producing fine tone quality and expression in exact synchronization with all the other performers.

Most of the warming up takes place backstage. To loosen up finger, hand, and lip muscles, each player goes through an individual routine that may take as much as twenty minutes.

About ten minutes before the start of the concert, players begin strolling out to their seats. Once they are on stage, another ritual occurs— the one the audience hears. The musicians adjust and test their instruments. Oboists squawk on their reeds, string players rosin and adjust their bows, and so on.

Then each musician plays his or her special onstage warm-up with apparent disregard for the other performers or the audience. Brass players test their double and triple tonguing, then explore their high and low tones; clarinetists and flutists run quick scales up and down; the timpanist taps and thumps on each of the large kettle drums; French horn players soar forth with passages from the upcoming performance; string players saw their bows back and forth across the strings—fingers flying up and down fingerboards. As each player joins the din, the sound evolves from minor chaos to total cacophony. And you thought you came to hear a concert by disciplined musicians!

The Concertmaster

Throughout this warming up, the first chair of the violin section is conspicuously empty. This chair is reserved for one of the orchestra's most important members—the concertmaster. As the chaotic sound on the stage gradually fades to silence, the concertmaster enters. For the first time, the audience applauds. The concertmaster stands next to his or her seat, violin in one hand and bow in the other, acknowledges the audience's applause, then turns and faces the orchestra. The concertmaster then signals the principal oboist to sound the traditional tuning pitch "A."

The Orchestra Tunes

Once the oboist sounds the "A," everyone in the orchestra gradually takes up the pitch—flutes in the high register; string basses, tubas, and bassoons in the low register. Tuning takes less than a minute. Without any signal, everyone suddenly stops, and there is silence on stage.

Why does the oboe sound the tuning pitch? First of all, the oboe player is usually seated near the middle of the orchestra, making it easy for everyone to hear. Second, the oboe's unique strident tone can be heard over the instruments. Third, the oboe is the least flexible instrument to tune. It has no tuning slides or pegs and relies for pitch on the length of its double reeds wrapped around a small pipe. Therefore, other instruments adjust to the oboe.

Today, some orchestras use an electronically produced "A" in place of the oboe because an electronic tuner sustains a constant pitch. And you will notice that the sound of the electronic tuner resembles that of an oboe.

If there's a piano already on stage for the soloist, the concertmaster will also play an "A" on the piano to be sure that the orchestra will be in tune with that instrument.

The Conductor Enters

As soon as the orchestra is quiet, the conductor crosses from the wings to the podium, usually through the violin section. The audience applauds a second time. After acknowledging the applause, the conductor mounts the podium and greets the concertmaster and the whole orchestra, often with a slight bow or nod. After looking around to be sure everyone is ready to play (no sense starting if a player is still fixing an instrument or shuffling music), the conductor waits for the audience to be quiet.

I have seen conductors turn around and glare at people not yet seated. Ushers usually close the doors and stop admitting people once the conductor has entered. When all is ready, the conductor raises his or her arms and gives the "downbeat" for the start of the concert.

Soloists

Soloists enter the stage only for the piece they will be playing or singing. Until they are on, they wait in a special room called the "green room." The room was once actually painted green in the belief that the color would relax performers, but today it can be any color. When it is time for the soloist's piece, the artist waits in the wings until the conductor comes to escort him or her through the orchestra to the front of the stage. Usually, the orchestra joins the audience in greeting the soloist with applause. String players often tap their bows on their stands to avoid setting the bows down.

The End of Each Piece on the Program

When a piece is finished, the conductor's arm and posture relax, and the audience applauds. Then the conductor turns to the audience to acknowledge the applause, personally and on behalf of the orchestra.

The conductor will allow a soloist to bow first. Conductor and orchestra then join the audience to applaud the soloist. After several bows, the soloist usually thanks the conductor with a handshake or embrace and leads the audience in applause for the conductor and orchestra. The soloist also shakes hands or bows to the concertmaster, and then nods to acknowledge the orchestra.

Tribute to Key Performers

While the applause continues, the conductor may motion to certain members of the orchestra to stand for applause. These were the key players or soloists for the music just performed.

Andre Previn, former conductor of The Los Angeles Philharmonic Orchestra (Courtesy
of The Los Angeles Philharmonic Orchestra)

Applause for the Whole Orchestra

The conductor will usually motion the entire orchestra to stand and
acknowledge the audience's applause. This may occur after any piece; however, it generally happens at the end of the concert.

The Performers Exit

If there is a soloist, the conductor motions the soloist to exit and then
follows. Otherwise, the conductor simply exits to the wings.

Reappearance of the Soloist and Conductor

Since applause usually continues after the first exit, the soloist re-enters
without the conductor for a solo bow and exit. If the applause continues, the
soloist and the conductor reappear together, the soloist leading the way.

Often the conductor and soloist hold hands. You see, artists are emotional people who touch and embrace on stage just like actors and dancers.
The orchestra, conductor, and soloist have worked together through many
intense hours of rehearsal leading to an exhausting performance. Now that
it is over and successful, they feel warm and gratified by having shared the
experience and the generosity of the audience's applause.

HOW WILL I KNOW WHEN TO APPLAUD?

Experienced concertgoers seem to know exactly when to clap, while newcomers often burst out in applause in the wrong places. If knowing the right moment seems a mystery, take heart. It is actually not difficult. A few simple guidelines will build your confidence.

> **GUIDELINE➡** WHEN IN DOUBT, WAIT TILL OTHERS APPLAUD.

If the music is unfamiliar, do not rush to applaud, no matter how moved you are. Also, wait until most of the audience is applauding as there may be quite a few who start at the wrong time. Applause between movements breaks the mood and continuity of the whole piece. The only exception is between movements of a concerto where the soloist has played so brilliantly that the audience feels uncontrollably exhilarated by the performance. This might occur right after the first movement since it usually contains a lively tempo.

Now, if you would like to lead the applause or just feel comfortable about applauding, here are the times:

SYMPHONY ORCHESTRA CONCERTS

- the concertmaster (first violinist) enters from the wings
- the conductor enters from the wings
- the soloist or soloists enter from the wings
- the orchestra concludes an *entire* piece on the program
  (There should be no applause between sections of the same piece.)
- the conductor signals the orchestra to stand at any time
- the conductor re-enters from the wings
- the soloist or soloists re-enter from the wings
- the return of any of the artists for applause

RECITALS AND CHAMBER MUSIC CONCERTS

- the performers enter
- entire works end (watch program)

- encores (not listed on the program) conclude

- the performers return for applause or to continue the program

OPERAS

- the conductor enters the orchestra pit

- the overture ends (Exception: In some very serious operas, applause would break the mood set by the overture. Be in tune with the mood, or use *GUIDELINE*.)

- the curtain rises on the stage and set (Exception: for some operas the curtain rises before the overture ends.)

- the star performers enter

- an aria, duet, trio, and so forth concludes (Use *GUIDELINE* here also till you get to know the music or the style very well.)

- the curtain comes down

- the soloists, conductor, stage manager, and sometimes the composer take bows (use up all your applause here)

Riccardo Muti, Music Director of The Philadelphia Orchestra (Courtesy of The Philadelphia Orchestra/photo by Steve J. Sherman)

WAGNERIAN OPERAS

- the conductor enters the orchestra pit (In Bayreuth, you won't be able to see the conductor because the pit is covered. Use *GUIDELINE*.)

- the curtain goes up in a few "cheerful" operas (For Wagner's serious operas the audience won't applaud when the curtain is raised. Use *GUIDELINE*.)

- the curtain falls

- the performers take bows

BALLET

- the conductor enters the orchestra pit

- the overture, if there is one, ends (Use *GUIDELINE*.)

- the curtain rises

- the prima ballerina or the star male dancer enters (Use *GUIDELINE*.)

- outstanding solo dancers conclude a dance (Use *GUIDELINE*.)

- the curtain falls

- the soloists bow

HOW DO I RECOGNIZE THE END OF THE MUSIC?

After you hear a piece a few times—especially Beethoven's symphonies—you'll remember the ending. To be prepared, listen in advance.

Clues are on the printed program, which customarily lists the major sections, or movements, of the music. For instance, most concertos have three movements:

   I   **Allegro** (fast)

  II   **Adagio** (slow)

 III   **Allegro** (fast)

Knowing this and seeing it in the printed program, you will be able to keep track of the music by paying attention to the tempo of each section. Most symphonies, with some exceptions, have four movements and are generally ordered as follows:

I   **Allegro** (fast)

II **Adagio** or **Andante** (slow)

III **Allegretto** (moderately fast dance style)

IV **Allegro** (fast)

Symphonies by Mozart, Haydn, Beethoven, Schumann, Brahms, and many other composers closely fit this format. A further clue: notice how each movement comes to a complete stop or conclusion.

Another indication will come from the conductor or soloist. At the end of movements, the conductor's arms remain raised. The performers relax slightly and often adjust their instruments. After the final note of a concerto, symphony, or sonata, the conductor lowers both arms and the orchestra noticeably relaxes. After a sonata or concerto, an instrumental soloist lowers the instrument. The difference between the slight relaxation and the final relaxation will be obvious to you. At the end of a piece, the soloist is tired because performing demands physical and mental concentration. Also, relaxing lets the audience know that the entire piece is over.

WHAT IF THE AUDIENCE DOESN'T LIKE THE MUSIC OR PERFORMANCE?

In North America you might hear some booing, but rarely. More commonly, people might leave or deliver only mild applause. After a recent concert, one of the performers said of the audience that evening, "They clapped with their gloves on." However, European audiences can be more vocal.

Most audiences are very polite to performers, but I have been at a few concerts when some were not so kind. Once was in New York City at an outdoor summer concert at Lewisohn Stadium, when a few people booed the piano soloist at the end of the performance. They were young and seemed to be piano students. I can't remember who that soloist was, because I haven't heard of him since.

Another incident was at La Scala Opera House (Teatro alla Scala) in Milan when the audience's constant heckling of a singer really shocked me. Groups of people seemed furious at the lead tenor in a performance of Verdi's *Il Trovatore*. Many Italians know every note and every word in Italian opera, and having heard many, many tenors sing those arias, they knew exactly when this tenor sang out of tune. That night, the tenor was certainly off. Each time he slipped, the audience shouted curses. They booed and hissed through the performance.

I was standing amid a crowd of the worst hecklers—yes, standing. The performance was sold out when I arrived in Milan, so I had to buy a standing-room ticket from a scalper. Since the standing-room spaces are the "cheapest seats," those who buy them often show up just to heckle and leave.

To be fair, most Italian opera lovers attend performances to cheer. And they frequently do. At a summer performance of *Andrea Chenier* in Verona, one man even cheered between lines of dialogue to show his great appreciation for soprano Montserrat Caballé and tenor José Carreras. He correctly cheered *brava* for the soprano, *bravo* for the tenor, and *bravi* for both of them.

Then there is the well-known incident involving the great Italian conductor, Arturo Toscanini, who had come to the United States during the 1930s to escape the Nazis. Soon he became the conductor of the New York Philharmonic Orchestra and later the NBC Symphony Orchestra. After World War II, he returned to his home town of Parma, Italy, as guest conductor of an opera.

He was not long into the pit when the audience began heckling the singers and the orchestra. Toscanini, having forgotten that heckling is a way of life in Parma, became outraged. When the audience started picking on the tenor (always the tenor), and shouting, "Go back to Rome, fatso!" Toscanini had enough. He stopped the performance, threw down his baton, reeled around to the audience and, before stomping out of the orchestra pit, shouted: "I'll never perform for you again, you . . .!"

The most infamous incident of a violent audience reaction, perhaps to any art work, occurred in Paris in 1913 at the first performance of Igor Stravinsky's *The Rite of Spring.* A large segment of the audience, objecting to the new, modern sounds of the music, began heckling. A fight broke out. Fists flew. Seats were ripped out and thrown. The fight spilled out into the Paris streets and was finally brought under control by the Paris Riot Squad. Heckling by the audience is becoming rare today—that role is now relegated to critics.

CAN I LEAVE IF I DON'T LIKE THE CONCERT?

Yes, of course you can. You are never obliged to suffer through any performance. If you really dislike the music and are very uncomfortable, leave!

Out of courtesy to the performers and to the rest of the audience, try to exit as inconspicuously as possible. Wait until a break in the music—at intermission, or the end of the work. These are the times you will disturb others least.

You can avoid disappointment if you know what to expect. Listen to a recording of the music in advance, and read as much as you can about the piece and the composer. If you still don't like the program, wait for a concert with music you do enjoy. As the scope of your enjoyment expands, you will probably come to appreciate a wider variety of music.

Since you are a ticket buyer, feel free to make your opinions known by writing a note to the concert management or performers. Ask for their addresses at the box office. Most performers and managers want to know how people feel about a performance, so they will take your letter seriously. Most of all, write when you enjoy the performance. Musicians never tire of acknowledgment.

Also, write to your newspaper about a concert or a published article. Your letter will help increase newspaper coverage. Newspapers attach importance and allot space to those areas of the arts that produce the most mail.

SHOULD I READ MUSIC CRITICS' REVIEWS?

Yes, but cautiously. Don't let anyone spoil your experience. The review might be published a day or two after a performance you attended. If you enjoyed it, who cares what some reviewer thought of it. Whether you liked it or not, your feelings are indisputable. Remember, a critic's review is just one person's judgment and may not reflect the audience's opinion. Some critics are indiscriminately nasty, feeling their duty is to find fault with all concerts. Of course, that's easy to do when you are dealing with live performances. Certainly, an occasional note will be blurred or a tempo rushed or some passage played too loudly or softly. But should those exceptions change your personal enjoyment?

On the other hand, some reviewers seem to like everything they hear and show no discernment. That's another story. Read those music critics who get to the heart of performances—those who understand great communication, not just technical perfection.

Also, beware of reviewers' jargon, which can intimidate non-musicians. Some critics feel compelled to show off their knowledge and musical background. If their arrogance insults you, write to them and to the editor of the newspaper. Let them know how you feel.

However, a reviewer may be such an excellent journalist that the commentary itself is entertainment—whether you agree with it or not. Here is a portion of an entertainingly written review by *Los Angeles Times'* music editor Martin Bernheimer of a concert conducted by the Los Angeles Philharmonic's former Music Director, Zubin Mehta.

Mehta Meets Strauss: *Superpow*

Bad music has always brought out the best in Zubin Mehta. Subtlety, elegance, introspection and understatement are not his things. *Piano* was never his forte.

But give the man a big, rumbling, snorting, slurping, soaring, whomping, thumping, zonking, rattling, repetitive challenge that builds reluctantly to a cataclysmic cadence, and watch out. Pow.

Make that superpow.

Zubin Mehta, guest conductor of The Israeli Philharmonic Orchestra (Courtesy of ICM Artists LTD./photo by Kathleen M. Hat)

The Los Angeles Philharmonic gave its former music director an ideal challenge—or allowed him to bring his own—Thursday night at the Dorothy Chandler Pavilion. The somewhat redundant program, devoted exclusively to music of Richard Strauss, climaxed with the "Symphony Domestica."

. . . The composer cranked out the decadent indulgence in a fit of egomania back in 1903. He felt the world simply had to know all about the mundane doings, comings and goings in the Strauss *Haus.*

With brilliant over-orchestration and a shameless ear for the magnified detail, the master painted an affectionate, presumably realistic, probably idealized, unabashedly vulgar tone-portrait of life at home with his much-loved, eminently shrewish wife, Pauline, and his much-loved, eminently adorable son, Bubi.

. . . The world cannot forget, however, that this was supposed to be his symphonic ode to the joys of marital squabbling, baby bathing, working, dreaming, waking and, yes, making love (no doubt a daring gambit for 1903). Posterity should be grateful, we suppose, that Strauss at least kept his bathroom door closed.

There is only one way to play the "Domestica," if it must be played at all. With whole-hearted conviction, with passion, with urgency, and with expressive grandeur.

Pretending the challenge was a deathless masterpiece, he [Mehta] inspired propulsive, extraordinarily precise and gratifyingly cohesive responses from the Philharmonic.

The heroic slush pump was in fine form . . .

Had you attended the same concert as Mr. Bernheimer, you might have come away with an entirely different reaction. Who would be right, you or a reviewer? You would both be right. The joy of music and of the arts is that each of us perceives a work differently, and there is no right or wrong.

2

THE PERFORMERS

THE CONDUCTOR

IS THE CONDUCTOR NECESSARY?

That depends on the size of the ensemble. For chamber music ensembles of ten or fewer players, no; for a symphony orchestra, yes (although I have heard musicians in orchestras express doubts about a particular conductor).

WHAT DOES THE CONDUCTOR DO?

Coordinating the ensemble's performance and interpreting the music are the conductor's responsibilities. The conductor's downbeat coordinates the start of the performance. The next beats set the tempo, with the orchestra or chorus following and watching for changes.

A soloist adds another dimension to a conductor's work because the orchestral accompaniment must be coordinated with the soloist's part. If, for instance, the soloist drags the tempo in a certain passage and speeds up in another, the conductor must inspire the entire orchestra to follow.

Christof Perick, Music Director of The Los Angeles Chamber Orchestra (Courtesy of The Los Angeles Chamber Orchestra/photo by Robert Millard)

Maintaining the balance between soloist and ensemble ensures that the soloist isn't drowned out. Watch the conductor during a soloist's performance and you will understand why the orchestra plays softer in many passages.

As you watch a conductor, you might get the impression that setting the tempo and beating time are the main functions. They aren't. Almost any member of the orchestra can do those things. Although beating time is important, interpreting the music is more so.

To understand how conductors convey interpretation, you would have to be on stage and watch how they use their hands, faces, and bodies to urge musicians to play louder or softer, more accented or more smoothly, tenderly or heroically. But even from that viewpoint you'd see only a small part of the conductor's role. Before rehearsals begin, the conductor thoroughly studies the conductor's score, known also as the full score. This contains all the parts exactly as the players see them. Having studied the score carefully, the conductor can spot any player's deviation from the music during rehearsals—where the real work takes place.

THE CONDUCTOR AS MUSIC SCHOLAR

It takes a lifetime of study for a conductor to learn all the great music literature for symphony orchestra, chorus, ballet, or opera. Guiding an ensemble to perform closest to a composer's intentions also requires that a
conductor research various sources and examine writing about the music.
Very revealing can be a composer's note to a colleague about a particular
piece. Many composers wrote essays or gave lectures about their music.
Sometimes the research of a music historian or analyst can provide additional insight. Conductors also give credence to other conductors' writings
about the music. Interpretation is a synthesis of insights by scholars and
performers.

Great music, as all great art, has an eternal fascination. One performance of Beethoven's Fifth Symphony is never like any other. Music is
timeless because each performance of a great masterpiece is unique; each
conductor and each ensemble makes an artistic contribution.

WHY DO SOME CONDUCTORS USE A BATON?

If you think of the baton as an extension of the conductor's arm, you will
understand why conductors use it. A baton allows players in all parts of the
ensemble to see the conductor's beats more clearly. This extension saves
the conductor from the exertion of arm flailing, or "carving" as André
Previn calls it.

Other objects besides a baton have been tried and discarded: rolled
up music, a stick, a cane. In the 17th century, Jean-Baptiste Lully (1632–
87) gave beats by pounding a large, wooden staff on the floor. During
one performance he accidentally smashed the staff into his foot. It became infected and he died of complications, thus ending the use of the
staff.

Using a baton isn't mandatory; many conductors do not use one.
Choral directors usually work without a baton because the director's facial
expressions, articulation of words, and hand movements are more important than beats.

HOW DO CONDUCTORS COMMUNICATE?

Most conductors use patterns universally recognized by classically trained
musicians and even by many folk and popular music conductors. These
standard patterns produce instant understanding, especially when the conductor is new to the ensemble. Once the performers and the conductor

become familiar with each other's idiosyncrasies, the patterns are less essential.

Imagine a guest conductor from Germany conducting the Chicago Symphony Orchestra featuring a guest soloist from Russia. It happens all the time. I once conducted in Berlin a massed-band concert which consisted of bands from the United States, France, Belgium, and Germany. Though we spoke different languages, we were able to perform together because all knew the standard conducting patterns and the universal language of music.

Ready to Play Position

The conductor mounts the podium, waits until everyone in the orchestra is ready to perform, then raises both arms in the *ready position*. (See Rilling photo.)

Downbeat

The first beat of any pattern is called the *downbeat*. The conductor moves the baton down from the ready position to a place in front of the body, near the waist. Cleveland Orchestra members used to joke about

Ready position—Helmuth Rilling, conductor (Courtesy of ICM Artists LTD./photo by Klaus Hennch)

the famous George Szell's down-beat because it was extremely vague. Ultimately they reacted when his baton reached the third shirt button from the top.

STANDARD CONDUCTING PATTERNS

Figure 2-1 shows the standard conducting patterns. Why are there different patterns? Patterns are determined by the *meter* or grouping of beats in the music. Most music is grouped in predictable patterns—usually two, three, and four.

The Two Pattern

Typically, marches use a pattern of 1–2, 1–2, which coordinates with marching left, right, left, right. To conduct a march, conductors use the *two pattern*. Try conducting the standard two pattern using recordings of the following pieces of music:

Bach	Brandenburg Concerto No. 2 [3rd movement], Allegro
Beethoven	Symphony No. 7 in A Major [2nd movement]
Gershwin	*An American in Paris* [opening section]
Mozart	Piano Concerto No. 21 (K. 467) [3rd movement]
Sousa	any march

The Three Pattern

Waltzes use a *three pattern:* 1–2–3, 1–2–3. Try conducting the standard three pattern to the following music:

Beethoven	Symphony No. 2 in D Major [2nd movement]
Mahler	Symphony No. 1 in D Major (*Titan*) [2nd movement]
Mozart	Symphony No. 35 in D Major (*Haffner*) [3rd movement]
Mozart	Symphony No. 36 in C Major (*Linz*) [3rd movement]

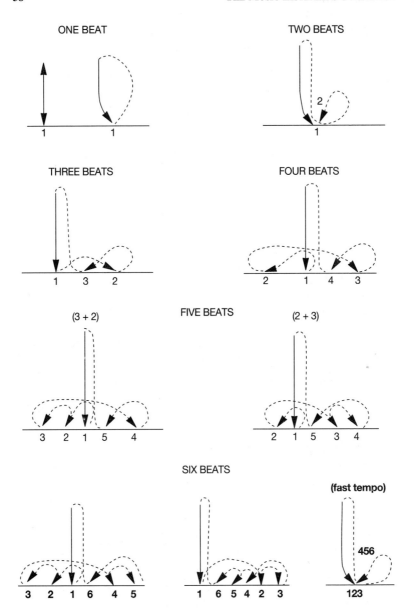

Figure 2-1   Standard Conducting Patterns

Mozart	Symphony No. 39 in E-Flat Major [3rd movement]
Mozart	Symphony No. 40 in g minor [3rd movement]
Mozart	Symphony No. 41 in C Major (*Jupiter*) [3rd movement]
Ravel	*Bolero*
Schubert	Symphony No. 8 in b minor (*Unfinished*) [both movements]
Tchaikovsky	Piano Concerto No. 1 in b-flat minor [1st movement]

The Four Pattern

Since so much music uses the *four pattern,* musicians call it "common time." Most popular music can be conducted with the four pattern, and here are some classical music pieces that use this pattern:

Beethoven	Piano Concerto No. 5 in E-Flat Major (*Emperor*) [1st movement]
Gershwin	*An American in Paris* [2nd section]
Mozart	Piano Concerto No. 21 in C Major [1st movement]

The Five Pattern

A less-frequently used meter and conducting pattern is the *five pattern.* Here are some pieces that use a five pattern:

| Holst | *The Planets* ("Mars") |
| Tchaikovsky | Symphony No. 6 in b minor (*Pathètique*) [2nd movement] |

Note in the pattern chart (Figure 2-1) the two patterns used to conduct the five grouping, depending on the music.

1–2–3   4–5 (used in Holst's *The Planets*)

1–2   3–4–5 (used in Tchaikovsky's Symphony No. 6)

John Williams conducting The Boston Pops Orchestra (Courtesy of The Boston Pops Orchestra/photo by Richard Feldman)

The Six Pattern

Occasionally, music uses a six pattern. The following pieces work well in this pattern:

Mendelssohn	Violin Concerto in e minor [2nd movement]
Mozart	Symphony No. 40 in g minor [2nd movement]

The Fast Six Pattern

When the six pattern moves very fast, it tends to group into a larger pattern of two:

fast: 1   2
slow: (1 – 2 – 3   4 – 5 – 6)

To conduct the faster six pattern, the conductor merely uses the simpler two pattern. Here are a few pieces of music using the fast six pattern, which you can conduct with the two pattern:

Beethoven	Symphony No. 6 in F Major (*Pastoral*) [5th movement]
Beethoven	Symphony No. 7 in A Major [1st movement]

Left-Hand Expression

The conductor's left hand indicates expression. For example, if the trumpets enter too loudly, the conductor, looking like a policeman halting traffic, motions them to play more softly. (See John Williams photo.)

Urging the violins to play more loudly, the conductor might also use a left-hand signal. (See Seiji Ozawa photo.)

Cueing

A conductor also uses the left hand to signal a player or a section to begin playing. Since music contains both sound and silence, some players make sounds and others, silence. Imagine a cymbal player who has been waiting fifteen minutes to crash his cymbals immediately after a very quiet section. Without the conductor's assistance, that crash could occur at the wrong moment—quite an embarrassing situation!

Seiji Ozawa, Music Director of The Boston Symphony Orchestra (Courtesy of The Boston Symphony Orchestra/photo by Steve J. Sherman)

Riccardo Muti, Music Director of The Philadelphia Orchestra
(Courtesy of The Philadelphia Orchestra/photo by Steve J. Sherman)

Body and Facial Gestures

A televised concert is a marvelous opportunity to see a conductor's facial expressions and body movements. The cameras zoom in on the most subtle eyebrow movements. You'll see what the performers see—expressions of approval, surprise, admiration, and occasionally anger. Of course, some conductors are aware of this intimacy and often play to the camera.

Each conductor has a distinctive style. Leonard Bernstein was known for his leaping, Herbert von Karajan for his crouching, and Michael Tilson Thomas for his dancing. Their gyrations are entertaining, but they don't affect the performance. What a contrast—the conductor having the equivalent of an aerobic workout, while the players hardly move. Some conductors are a joy to watch: George Solti, Zubin Mehta, Seiji Ozawa, JoAnn Falletta, Riccardo Muti, and Claudio Abbado to name a few.

SYMPHONY ORCHESTRA PERFORMERS

The symphony orchestra is a marvel of human achievement. Each member functions both independently and as a part of the group. Musical parts must fit together precisely, much like a jigsaw puzzle. Performers feel a great respect for each other and, above all, share complete trust.

HOW DO THEY KNOW WHEN TO PLAY? Seasoned professionals know exactly when to play. But until they gain that experience, they must methodically count beats and measures. For instance, if the trombones have a four-measure rest, and the piece is in the meter of three, they have 12 beats to count (4 measures of 3 beats = 12 beats). The trombonists count:

$$\boxed{\mathbf{1} - 2 - 3, \mathbf{2} - 2 - 3, \mathbf{3} - 2 - 3, \mathbf{4} - 2 - 3, \textbf{ play} \atop \uparrow}$$

The first number (in larger type) of each group shows the measure they are on; the other numbers, the rest of the beats in that measure. The conductor helps by indicating entrance cues, but in case he or she gets carried away with the flow of the music and forgets to cue, the trombones enter on their own.

I played trumpet for a recording and a performance of the Berlioz *Requiem*. The music calls for four groups of brass players in different locations around the hall. I was with the group in the balcony where the

JoAnn Falletta, Music Director of The Long Beach Symphony (California) (Courtesy of The Long Beach Symphony Orchestra/photo by Alex Köster)

conductor could not see us. Harry Glantz, my stand partner, had played first trumpet for many years with the NBC Symphony under Toscanini. During rehearsals, Harry delighted in distracting us by telling jokes. His timing was perfect. He would deliver the punchline, pick up his trumpet, and play right on cue—never missing a beat.

CONCERTMASTER

The first violinist holds this position. Regarded as the next in importance to the conductor, the concertmaster is greeted with applause. The concertmaster's duties are manifold: assisting the conductor in matters of interpretation and style, stepping in for the conductor in an emergency, conducting at children's concerts, making orchestra personnel decisions in conjunction with the conductor, and tuning the orchestra. As leader of the violin section, the concertmaster performs all the solo violin passages in the music.

In the 17th century, the concertmaster often stood by his seat and indicated beats with his bow while the conductor (usually the composer) sat at the keyboard. Everyone in the orchestra could see the violinist's bow. In fact, many early conductors used a violin bow instead of a baton.

The final word on bowing comes from the concertmaster. During rehearsals, the players pencil the concertmaster's directions into their music.

Seiji Ozawa, Music Director of The Boston Symphony Orchestra (Courtesy of The Boston Symphony Orchestra)

When in doubt they glance at the concertmaster and follow. Bowing style and direction have to be carefully planned. If all the bows do not move together, it could be distracting, and the tone might vary among the violinists.

ROLES OF PRINCIPAL PLAYERS OR SECTION LEADERS

Concert programs list the orchestra personnel and indicate the principal players or section leaders. For instance, a French horn section may contain four players, with one designated "principal," or "first horn," and the others designated "second," "third," and "fourth horn." Besides playing most of the solo passages, the section leader decides which mutes, special effects, and articulation to use, as well as other performance concerns.

THE STANDARD ORCHESTRA

With minor variations, today's orchestras employ musicians on a full-time basis, and most utilize the same number and type of instruments. Unusual or additional instruments are brought in as needed. You will notice the great orchestras such as the Chicago Symphony, Boston Symphony, Berlin Philharmonic, and London Symphony have similar seating arrangements. A typical seating plan is shown in Figure 2-2.

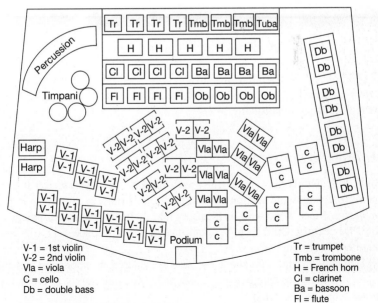

Figure 2-2 Typical Symphony Orchestra Seating Arrangement.

THE SECTIONS OF THE ORCHESTRA

The four main sections in the symphony orchestra are the string, woodwind, brass, and percussion.

STRING SECTION

The string section has historically been the most important, partly because of the earlier development of the instruments. Beginning about 1650, the great craftsmen of Cremona, Italy—Stradivari, Amati, and Guarneri—created the finest instruments ever constructed.

The string section in today's orchestra typically contains:

First Violins	18
Second Violins	16
Violas	12
Cellos	12
Basses	8

By about 1740, when string instruments had reached their peak of development, woodwind and brass instruments were still crude. Toward the end of the 18th century, woodwind, brass, and percussion instruments began challenging the dominance of the strings. Today, most composers treat all four sections equally.

WOODWIND SECTION

Since woodwinds play more softly than the brass and percussion instruments, the woodwind section is just behind the strings in the center of the orchestra. Most woodwind instruments had their modern development in the 19th century. Until then, the instruments could produce only a limited number of notes and keys.

Although the saxophone is also considered a woodwind instrument, it is more frequently used in jazz styles and only rarely in orchestral music.

The Montréal Symphony Orchestra, Charles Dutoit, Music Director (Courtesy of ICM Artists Ltd.)

The following woodwind instruments are typical of an orchestra woodwind section for late 19th-century compositions by such composers as Richard Strauss and Richard Wagner:

Piccolo	1
Flutes	2–4
Oboes	2–4
English horn	1
High E-flat clarinet	1
Clarinets	2–4
Bass clarinet	1
Bassoons	2–4
Contrabassoon	1

BRASS SECTION

Because the brass instruments are loud, brass players usually sit behind the woodwinds, toward the rear of the stage. Until the middle of the 19th century, composers used brass instruments sparingly. But once valves were added to the trumpets, French horns, and tubas, the brass section became an important part of the orchestra. A typical modern orchestration calls for the following brass instruments:

Trumpets	4
French horns	4–6
Trombones	4
Bass trombone	1
Tuba	1

PERCUSSION SECTION

In the 18th century, the percussion section consisted of only timpani—usually one pair. During the 19th century, cymbals, bass drums, snare drums, and additional timpani became part of the standard orchestra to heighten the excitement of the music. It wasn't till the 20th century, however, that composers more fully explored the unique sounds and interesting possibilities of the percussion section.

Today the percussion section contains a wide variety of instruments: gongs, chimes, bells, xylophones, tambourines, castanets, triangles, rattles, drums of all sizes, timpani or "kettle drums," and a host of exotic instruments borrowed from cultures around the world. George Gershwin, for instance, used a set of taxi horns in *An American in Paris* to replicate the sounds and the flavor of Parisian traffic in the 1920s.

Since percussionists usually play more than one instrument and move from one to another, the percussion section occupies a large area at the rear or side of the orchestra. Today's standard orchestra uses the following percussion instruments:

Cymbals	1 player
Snare drum	1 or 2 players
Bass drum	1 player
Timpani	1 player
Chimes, marimba, bells, xylophone	1 or 2 players
Triangle and assorted instruments	1 player

OTHER INSTRUMENTS

Some music calls for one or two harps, and occasionally a piano, organ, celesta, or harpsichord. Since these aren't considered part of any particular section, they're usually placed at the side of the orchestra.

HOW CAN I BECOME FAMILIAR WITH THE INSTRUMENTS?

Associating the instruments you see at concerts with the sounds they produce is the best way to become familiar with them. Two marvelous pieces of music introduce the instruments of the orchestra:

Benjamin Britten   *The Young Person's Guide to the Orchestra*

Serge Prokoviev   *Peter and the Wolf*

Composers have written concertos for every instrument including guitar, timpani, tuba, and even piccolo. After you listen to a solo concerto, you will recognize each instrument's unique qualities.

WHAT TRAINING DO THE PERFORMERS HAVE?

Musicians are highly trained specialists, many of whom begin studying their instruments as early as age three or four. I once asked my piano teacher, Leopold Mittman, the famous accompanist and soloist, why he chose the piano. He looked puzzled at the question, then answered, "I had no choice. Everyone in my family was a musician. My brothers and sisters were violinists, violists, and cellists. They needed a pianist."

At a very early age, a person reveals genius mainly in three fields: chess, mathematics, and music. Mozart was a touring concert performer on piano and violin by the age of six. Many other great musicians displayed their virtuosity in concerts by eight, nine, or ten years of age: Ludwig van Beethoven, Felix Mendelssohn, Frédéric Chopin, Franz Liszt.

But talent is only a part of the successful musician's background: years of lessons and hours and hours of daily practice are the other elements. Concert pianist Rosalyn Tureck, a Bach specialist, once told me, "I try to practice eight hours a day when I'm not traveling." Eight hours a day of Bach! What concentration and dedication!

European musicians usually enter a conservatory of music while in their teens. After spending a whole day at their regular school, they study their main instrument, secondary instruments, conducting, theory, and orchestration at the conservatory.

In the United States, the conservatory education for young musicians is relatively new. Those with professional aspirations begin studying their main instrument through private instruction. After graduating from high school, they may enter a school of music or music conservatory within a college or university where they can major in music and take liberal arts courses.

Today's schools of music prepare students better than ever for careers in music. Here are some of the prominent North American schools:

Curtis Institute of Music

Indiana University School of Music

Juilliard School of Music

McGill University School of Music

New England Conservatory of Music

Northwestern University School of Music

Oberlin College Conservatory of Music

Peabody Conservatory of Music

University of British Columbia School of Music

University of Miami School of Music

University of Michigan School of Music

University of Rochester Eastman School of Music

University of Southern California School of Music

University of Toronto School of Music

These excellent schools have highly regarded symphony orchestras which rival many professional orchestras. Also, their excellent wind ensembles, choirs, opera companies, and chamber music ensembles compare favorably with the best in the world.

Standards for entrance into the schools of music are extremely high: candidates must be excellent vocal or instrumental performers. Then for the next four years, to complete a bachelor of music degree, they study

Isaac Stern, violinist (Courtesy of ICM Artists Ltd.)

music theory, analysis of music, music history, orchestration, conducting, their major instrument, and usually piano. In addition, the students regularly perform in recitals and concerts.

For many aspiring musicians, college is an opportunity to play with other highly talented performers, and the competition is keen. Students who were the best in their high schools find themselves among the best from schools around the world. They must constantly perform for each other and audition for positions in the bands, choirs, orchestras, and opera companies. These experiences prepare them for their professional careers.

AUDITIONING FOR A PROFESSIONAL ORCHESTRA

Dedicated and thorough training prepares an orchestral musician to become a working member of an orchestra. Vacant positions are advertised in professional journals and notices are sent to schools of music. As many as two hundred musicians might audition for one position in a professional orchestra.

First, applicants send audio tapes to a committee of orchestra members for the preliminary screening. This process reduces the candidate pool to those invited to audition in person.

DO ORCHESTRA PERFORMERS STILL NEED TO PRACTICE?

They certainly do. Daily. Professionals have to maintain their performance skills and physical and mental condition to keep their positions. Conductors, management, audiences, and fellow musicians all expect players to perform at their best. An oboist who squawks a tone, a horn player who bloops a note, or a violinist who scrapes the bow can detract from an otherwise excellent performance.

Being a member of a major symphony orchestra is not a part-time job. It demands an artist's full dedication. These orchestras perform year round, including summer festivals, tours, and recordings. With such a demanding schedule, the performers cannot afford to get out of shape.

Many performances have little slips—musicians are human. But the slips are usually so slight that only the other musicians notice. While playing second trumpet with the American Opera Society Orchestra in Carnegie Hall, I played a note slightly off-pitch. One of the horn players turned around and glared at the first trumpet thinking he was the culprit. Nobody else seemed to notice—not even the conductor. I, of course, just kept playing.

WHAT ABOUT TOURING?

Touring is an interesting and sometimes agonizing fact of life for a musician. One thing is sure: touring is not all glamorous.

Yo-Yo Ma, cellist, and Emanuel Ax, pianist (Courtesy of ICM Artists Ltd.)

Transporting instruments is a major concern. Some are too valuable to travel in the cargo bay of an aircraft. Many rare instruments could not be replaced if damaged or stolen. Therefore, violinists carry their Strads with them at all times. Cellists must pay an additional half or full fare for their instruments, which are strapped in the seat next to them. There is a lot of waiting—in airports, in train stations, in hotel lobbies.

After a long trip, sitting on a metal folding chair during a two-hour performance is not very comfortable. But touring carries the musician's art to enthusiastic audiences, and the smiles and applause make it worthwhile.

GUEST SOLOISTS

Audiences flock to hear guest soloists perform with their local symphony orchestra. The most popular soloists are pianists, violinists, cellists, and singers. Such soloists as Vladimir Ashkenazy, Andre Watts, Itzhak Perlman, Roger Kennedy, Midori, Lynn Harrell, Luciano Pavarotti, and Kathleen Battle appear regularly with major orchestras throughout the world.

Singers may perform several operatic arias. Instrumental soloists usually perform only one major work on each program—a concerto. They appear at rehearsals and the concert only for that piece. It sounds easy, but it isn't. The audience expects to be thrilled by the soloist, not just satisfied. After waiting in the green room for an hour, the soloist comes on stage and turns on the brilliance for only thirty minutes. It takes a highly talented performer to do that one hundred or more times a year.

WHOSE INTERPRETATION AND TEMPO PREVAIL?

That decision depends on the soloist and the conductor. A venerated, master violinist such as Isaac Stern playing Mendelssohn's Violin Concerto, for example, will have almost total control, with the conductor following in both tempo and style. Younger soloists discuss tempo and interpretation with the conductor before rehearsals with the full orchestra.

Friction occasionally occurs between well-known soloists and equally well-known conductors. I have witnessed these artistic tugs-of-war when the conductor sets one tempo and the soloist ignores it. At a concert by the London Symphony Orchestra in the Royal Festival Hall, I watched the orchestra completely run away from the soloist. That a disagreement had occurred was obvious to everyone. The conductor was the late Thomas Shippers. The soloist, still performing, will remain anonymous.

Give and take between artists creates some of the excitement of live performances. Each has studied the music honestly and carefully, and sometimes each has a slightly different conception and approach. These differences make art interesting.

Watch these roles carefully at your next concert. See if the conductor and soloist maintain the same tempo and styles. Notice how they glance at each other—even the way they take their bows. Does the conductor bow only politely to the soloist or do they embrace?

RECITAL PERFORMERS

Most artists are at their best in a recital, performing their favorite works in a small hall for a highly appreciative audience. These experiences are among the high points in artists' lives.

Many famous artist-teachers purposely establish a double career for themselves so they can continue to display their talent to a wide audience. Since they are constantly working on recital literature with their students, they want to perform that literature themselves.

HOW DO RECITALISTS PREPARE?

Maybe you have heard the joke about a young musician who stopped an old man on the street in New York City and asked, "How do I get to Carnegie Hall?" The man answered, "Practice, my son, practice!" That is the truth. The recitalist strives for perfection, practicing small runs and fast passages over and over. Until a passage can be played smoothly and comfortably, the performer plays it slowly, then begins repeating it faster and faster—like a race driver trying to find that optimum speed to hit a turn, but not too fast to run off the road.

Performers want the technical side of the music—the quick finger and hand movements—to become automatic. That frees musicians to add the layers of nuances, phrasing, and expression that make for real artistry. Attaining prominence requires a great deal of hard work. The "think system" of Professor Harold Hill in *The Music Man* (just thinking about playing the music without developing skills through practicing) does not really work.

For young artists, recitals (and competitions) are the route to becoming known in the concert world. Artist management agencies do everything possible to secure bookings and media reviews to publicize that their young clients have the right stuff for a solo career.

Almost all music schools require students to perform recitals. To prepare for my recitals at the Oberlin Conservatory of Music, I practiced seven hours a day and studied summers with the first trumpet player of the New York Philharmonic. Seven hours a day works the lips, or "embouchure," overtime. But to use a phrase from William Blake, "You never know what is enough, unless you know what is too much." (Proverbs from *Marriage Between Heaven and Hell.*)

WHAT IS THE ROLE OF THE ACCOMPANIST?

The ideal relationship between accompanist and soloist is an artistic collaboration. At your next recital, try focusing on just the soloist and then switch your attention to the accompanist. Watch the two together as they subtly communicate to each other.

Most great composers wrote equally important parts for piano and for soloists, and in fact, many composers performed those piano parts themselves—Bach, Mozart, Schubert, Schumann, Brahms, and Debussy to name a few. Beethoven marked his sonatas, Sonata for Violin and Piano, not Violin and Piano Accompaniment. Other composers do the same.

After two artists have rehearsed long hours together to perfect their performance, they develop mutual respect for each other's musicianship and often perform as a team for years. Leopold Mittman concertized with violinist Nathan Milstein for 12 years and with violinist Mischa Elman for nine years. Brooks Smith appeared with violinist Jascha Heifetz over forty years.

Dalton Baldwin has worked with French singer Pierre Bernac for over thirty-five years. Bernac was so impressed with the ease of their first collaboration that he persuaded Baldwin to leave his studies at Oberlin College and tour with him as his regular accompanist. They've been together ever since.

Accompanist Martin Katz and singer Marilyn Horne met as classmates at the School of Music of the University of Southern California. Both were studying with the great vocal coach and professor of accompaniment, Gwendolyn Koldofsky. They are still working together.

Some accompanists are also coaches. Leopold Mittman, after touring with many great artists, decided to settle in New York City and coach young performers. He accompanied and coached such artists as violinists Michael Rabin and Ruggiero Ricci, and cellist David Soyer. Their Carnegie Hall and Town Hall recitals were some of my earliest musical experiences, for Mittman asked me to don a tuxedo and turn pages for him during their performances.

CHAMBER MUSIC PERFORMERS

WHY DO MUSICIANS PERFORM CHAMBER MUSIC?

Many performers prefer playing chamber music because of their close interaction with the other players and the individual decision making. Symphony players defer these decisions to the conductor. Not so in a chamber group, where each member contributes.

Besides, it is also more fun to rehearse and tour with a small group—a string quartet or woodwind quintet—than with a large ensemble. When not rehearsing and performing with their orchestras, many musicians also play in chamber music ensembles—brass quintets, woodwind quintets, and string quartets. Occasionally, ten or fifteen members get together as a chamber orchestra. Performing chamber music allows musicians to make more of their own decisions on musical interpretation. It also allows each player a chance to be heard and to become a soloist.

DO SOME MUSICIANS PLAY ONLY CHAMBER MUSIC?

Yes, many do. Such groups as the Juilliard Quartet, Kronos Quartet, and the Canadian Brass Ensemble play chamber music exclusively as their full-time performing career.

The Chicago Brass Ensemble (Courtesy of The Chicago Chamber Brass)

3

THE MUSIC

The concert is about to begin, so let's talk about the music you will be hearing. Composers put their music in packages called *form*. Each musical composition, like a building, has an outer structure and a detailed inner structure. By knowing the structure or plan, you will have an idea of what to expect, and you will be able to keep your place in the music during the concert.

WHAT ARE THE TYPICAL LARGE FORMS USED IN CLASSICAL MUSIC?

FORMS USED IN ORCHESTRAL MUSIC

The Symphony

When we think of music for orchestra, we think of it first at its grandest—the *symphony,* a large, complex work. The symphony may be of any length: Webern's symphony lasts only ten minutes; many symphonies by Haydn and Mozart last from twenty to twenty-five minutes; a Mahler symphony may last up to ninety minutes.

Seiji Ozawa, Music Director of The Boston Symphony Orchestra (Courtesy of The Boston Symphony Orchestra)

The Symphony Plan	
First Movement	*Fast* (Allegro) [Optional: slow introduction]
Second Movement	*Slow* (Adagio, Andante, or similar tempo)
Third Movement	*Moderately fast* (Allegretto or Menuetto)
Fourth Movement	*Fast* (Allegro)

Occasionally, a slow introduction opens the symphony, preceding the *Allegro*. Josef Haydn (1732–1809) began using slow introductions in his symphonies to let his audiences at the Esterházy court outside Vienna know that the concert was starting. Since Haydn's concerts were often the guests' after-dinner entertainment, the introduction allowed them to find their seats leisurely in the music salon.

FIRST MOVEMENT: Fast (Allegro). First movements are generally the most serious because audiences have the energy and interest to follow the music through a complicated symphonic journey.

SECOND MOVEMENT: Slow (Adagio). Melody is what most audiences enjoy, and the second movement is the composer's opportunity to allow the orchestra to soar with beautiful melodies. Here the audience can sit back and listen to less complicated, songlike music shaped mostly by strings and woodwinds. The brass and percussion often rest here or have little to play.

THIRD MOVEMENT: Moderately fast, dance style (Allegretto). Since the minuet and the Austrian dance, the Ländler, were extremely popular at court in the time of Mozart and Haydn, composers purposely catered to their audience's taste for this dance style music. More recent composers used a similar style even though the music was meant for listening instead of dancing. Beethoven called this movement "scherzo" in eight of his nine symphonies.

FOURTH MOVEMENT: Fast (Allegro). Usually the mood of this fastest movement in the symphony is happy and triumphant. Much like the last act of a play, this movement brings everything together for resolution. The full orchestra gives its all in a brilliant finale.

Selected Listening

Beethoven	Symphony No. 1 in C Major
Beethoven	Symphony No. 2 in D Major
Beethoven	Symphony No. 3 in E-Flat Major (*Eroica*)
Beethoven	Symphony No. 5 in c minor
Beethoven	Symphony No. 7 in A Major
Bizet	Symphony No. 1 in C Major
Brahms	Symphony No. 1 in c minor
Brahms	Symphony No. 1 in D Major
Brahms	Symphony No. 3 in F Major
Dvořák	Symphony No. 9 in e minor (*New World*)
Haydn	Symphony No. 88 in G Major
Haydn	Symphony No. 94 in G Major (*Surprise*)
Haydn	Symphony No. 101 in D Major (*Clock*)
Haydn	Symphony No. 104 in D Major (*London*)

Isaac Stern, violinist (Courtesy of ICM Artists LTD./Photo by William T. Haroutounian)

Mahler	Symphony No. 1 in D Major (*Titan*)
Mahler	Symphony No. 4 in G Major
Mendelssohn	Symphony No. 3 in g minor (*Scottish*)
Mendelssohn	Symphony No. 4 in A Major (*Italian*)
Mozart	Symphony No. 35 in D Major (*Haffner*)
Mozart	Symphony No. 38 in D Major (*Prague*)
Mozart	Symphony No. 40 in g minor
Mozart	Symphony No. 41 in C Major (*Jupiter*)
Prokofiev	Symphony No. 1 in D Major (*Classical*)
Prokofiev	Symphony No. 5
Schubert	Symphony No. 9 in C Major (*Great*)
Schumann	Symphony No. 1 in B-Flat Major (*Spring*)
Shostakovich	Symphony No. 5
Sibelius	Symphony No. 2 in D Major
Tchaikovsky	Symphony No. 4 in f minor
Tchaikovsky	Symphony No. 5 in e minor

The Concerto

Many composers wrote concertos to display their virtuosity as soloists. Until music publishing became widespread in the nineteenth century, composers did not have access to other composers' works. They had to write their own display pieces to earn a living. Mozart, for instance, was the darling of the central European music world from the age of eight, when he began composing and playing his piano concertos. Beethoven also combined his pianistic and composing abilities to create five superb concertos for piano and orchestra.

Overall Concerto Plan

Take out the dance movement of a symphony and you have a concerto plan:

The Concerto Plan	
First Movement	*Moderately fast* (Allegro)
Second Movement	*Slow* (Adagio, Andante, or similar tempo)
Third Movement	*Fast* (Allegro)

FIRST MOVEMENT: Fast. This is similar in style to the first movement of a symphony. The difference is that a concerto usually includes a *cadenza,* a solo passage without the orchestra. Until Beethoven's time, soloists improvised these cadenzas at the time of the performance (a feature later used in jazz). When the soloist was also the composer, the performance usually went well. But when other soloists interjected their own styles, the cadenzas were poorly constructed and often out of character with the rest of the music. Beethoven wanted none of that. He was so angered by the mistreatment of his music by other soloists that he completely notated the cadenzas, thereby eliminating the possibility of improvisation. From then on, notation was standard practice.

SECOND MOVEMENT: Slow. This melodious, songlike movement was intended to showcase the soloist's ability to display warmth and feeling, with the orchestra held in the background.

THIRD MOVEMENT: Fast. The last movement displays the soloist's technique. Fast, brilliant playing and interplay with the orchestra make this

movement a lively contrast to the others. Very often the soloist has another
cadenza here, planned to dazzle the audience.

Selected Listening

Beethoven	Piano Concerto No. 3 in c minor
Beethoven	Piano Concerto No. 5 in E-Flat Major (*Emperor*)
Beethoven	Violin Concerto in D Major
Brahms	Piano Concerto No. 1 in d minor
Brahms	Violin Concerto in D Major
Chopin	Piano Concerto No. 2 in f minor
Dvořák	Cello Concerto in b minor
Gershwin	*Rhapsody in Blue*
Gershwin	Piano Concerto in F Major
Grieg	Piano Concerto in a minor
Haydn	Trumpet Concerto in E-Flat Major
Liszt	Piano Concerto No. 1 in E-Flat Major
Mendelssohn	Violin Concerto in e minor
Mozart	Horn Concerto No. 1 in D Major
Mozart	Horn Concerto No. 2 in E-Flat Major
Mozart	Horn Concerto No. 3 in E-Flat Major
Mozart	Horn concerto No. 4 in E-Flat Major
Mozart	Piano Concerto No. 15 in d minor
Mozart	Piano Concerto No. 21 in C Major
Prokofiev	Piano Concerto No. 1 in D-Flat Major
Rachmaninoff	Piano Concerto No. 2 in c minor
Schumann	Piano Concerto in a minor
Tchaikovsky	Piano Concerto No. 1 in b-flat minor
Tchaikovsky	Violin Concerto in D Major
Vivaldi	*The Four Seasons*

Concerto Grosso

The concerto grosso, or "grand concerto," developed in the Baroque
style period (1600–1750), characteristically featured several soloists and a
small string orchestra. Vivaldi and Telemann wrote many fine concerti
grossi, but perhaps the most popular are Bach's Six Brandenburg
Concertos, each concerto featuring different instruments.

Mozart called his multiple-soloist works "symphonie concertante."
Brahms and Beethoven included the names of the instruments in the titles,

such as Concerto for Violin and Cello, and Concerto for Piano, Violin, Cello, and Orchestra.

Concerto Grosso Plan

The concerto grosso has the same form as the solo concerto: Fast—Slow—Fast.

Selected Listening

Bach	*Brandenburg* Concerto No. 2 in F Major
Bach	*Brandenburg* Concerto No. 5 in D Major
Beethoven	Concerto for Piano, Violin, Cello and Orchestra in C Major
Brahms	Concerto for Violin and Cello in a minor
Handel	Concerto Grosso in d minor Opus 6 No. 10
Mozart	Symphonie Concertante for Oboe, Clarinet, Bassoon, Horn and Strings in E-Flat Major

The Opera Overture (Prelude)

Think of the overture to a Broadway musical, and you will understand the purpose and impact of the opera overture: to introduce the catchiest tunes and to stir the audience's anticipation. Mozart, Beethoven, Rossini, Verdi, Wagner, and other opera composers wrote stirring overtures that you will often find on symphony orchestra programs. In fact, many overtures have outlived their original operas.

Opera Overture Plan

The plans vary. Since the overture usually contains many themes from the opera, the composer arranges the music to show several contrasting moods and styles.

Selected Listening

Beethoven	Overture to *Fidelio*
Beethoven	*Leonore* Overture No. 1
Beethoven	*Leonore* Overture No. 2
Beethoven	*Leonore* Overture No. 3
Gershwin	Overture to *Porgy and Bess*
Lalo	Overture to *Le Roi d'Ys*
Mozart	Overture to *Don Giovanni*

Mozart	Overture to *The Magic Flute*
Mozart	Overture to *The Marriage of Figaro*
Mussorgsky	Prelude to *Khovantchina*
Rossini	*William Tell* Overture
Wagner	Overture to *Die Meistersinger von Nürnberg*
Wagner	Overture to *The Flying Dutchman*
Wagner	Prelude to *Lohengrin*
Wagner	Prelude and Love-Death from *Tristan and Isolde*
Weber	Overture to *Der Freischütz*
Weber	Overture to *Oberon*

The Concert Overture

Nineteenth-century composers developed orchestral pieces known as concert overtures. They make very appealing fillers on programs by providing contrast to the longer and more serious symphonies.

Some concert overtures stand completely alone from any other production. The designation is often used for a short orchestral work—Brahms' *Academic Festival Overture* fits this category.

Some concert overtures contain music from ballet scores or incidental music used in plays. Beethoven's overture to *The Creatures of Prometheus* was for a ballet, and his overture for *Egmont* was used as an introduction to his friend Goethe's play. Mendelssohn was so inspired after reading Shakespeare's *A Midsummer Night's Dream* that he wrote an overture without a specific production in mind. Later he added incidental music for an actual production.

Concert Overture Plan

Because the concert overture usually has many sections, it often uses the "free-sectional" form. Like the opera overture, no specific plan can be called typical.

Selected Listening

Beethoven	*Coriolan* Overture
Beethoven	*Egmont* Overture
Beethoven	*The Creatures of Prometheus* Overture
Berlioz	*Roman Carnival Overture*

Brahms	*Academic Festival Overture*
Brahms	*Tragic Overture*
Copland	*An Outdoor Overture*
Dvořák	*Carnival Overture*
Grieg	Concert Overture *In Autumn*
Mendelssohn	Overture to *A Midsummer Night's Dream*
Mendelssohn	*Hebrides Overture (Fingal's Cave)*
Rimsky-Korsakov	*Russian Easter Overture*
Schubert	*Rosamunde* Overture
Schumann	Overture to Schiller's *Bride of Messina*
Schumann	*Overture, Scherzo and Finale*
Tchaikovsky	*1812 Overture*
Tchaikovsky	*Romeo and Juliet* Overture-Fantasia

The Suite

The suite from the Baroque period consists of a set group of dance-style movements:

allemande	*sarabande*
courante	*gigue*

You will sometimes find these additional dance movements in the Baroque suite:

gavotte	*polonaise*
bourrée	*rigaudon*

Selected Listening

Bach	Orchestral Suite No. 1 in C Major
Bach	Orchestral Suite No. 2 in b minor
Bach	Orchestral Suite No. 3 in D Major
Handel	Suite from *The Royal Fireworks Music*
Handel	Suite from *The Water Music*

In later style periods, the suite developed into a group of loosely related pieces. Many suites are excerpts arranged for concert performance from stage music, film scores, or ballets.

Selected Listening

Bernstein	Suite from *West Side Story*
Bizet	Suite from *Carmen*
Bizet	*L'Arlésienne* Suite No. 1
Bizet	*L'Arlésienne* Suite No. 2
Borodin	"Polovtsian Dances" from *Prince Igor*
Copland	Suite from *Billy the Kid*
Copland	Suite from *Rodeo*
Falla	Suite from *El amor brujo*
Falla	Dances from *The Three-Cornered Hat*
Khachaturian	*Gayne* Ballet Suite
Milhaud	*Suite française*
Prokofiev	*Scythian Suite*
Prokofiev	*Lieutenant Kijé Suite*
Prokofiev	Suite from *The Love for Three Oranges*
Ravel	*Daphnis and Chloé* Suite
Rimsky-Korsakov	*Scheherazade*
Stravinsky	*Firebird* Suite
Stravinsky	*Petrushka* Suite
Tchaikovsky	*The Nutcracker* Suite
Williams	Suite from *Star Wars*

The Toronto Symphony Orchestra's string section (Courtesy of The Toronto Symphony Orchestra/Photo by Larry Miller)

Program Music

In descriptive orchestra works inspired by a story or idea, the music follows the story closely. Richard Strauss's *Don Juan* and *Death and Transfiguration* are examples. So convinced was Richard Strauss that enjoying the music depended on knowing the story it was based on, he insisted the scenario appear in the printed program. (These stories are not the same as "program notes," which give background information about a composition.)

Program music was a special feature of the nineteenth century. New concert audiences from the rising middle class were not as well schooled in listening to music as the highly educated aristocratic audiences of the eighteenth century. When the music closely followed a story, audiences had a frame of reference.

Program Music Plan

Here again, the mood and style change to fit the story—the glue that holds the work together.

Selected Listening

Berlioz	*Harold in Italy*
Berlioz	*Symphonie fantastique*
Dukas	*The Sorcerer's Apprentice*
Liszt	*Dante Symphony*
Liszt	*Faust Symphony*
Liszt	*Les Préludes*
Strauss, R.	*Ein Heldenleben (A Hero's Life)*
Strauss, R.	*Thus Spake Zarathustra (Also sprach Zarathustra)*
Strauss, R.	*Death and Transfiguration (Tod und Verklärung)*
Strauss, R.	*Don Juan*
Strauss, R.	*Till Eulenspiegel's Merry Pranks (Till Eulenspiegels lustige Streiche)*

Descriptive Music

Many works have titles that are descriptive of the piece's general theme, such as Beethoven's *Pastoral* Symphony (No. 6), Schumann's *Spring* Symphony (No. 1), and Vivaldi's *The Four Seasons*. Unlike program music, descriptive music has no detailed story. Nineteenth century composers followed the trend of giving their works descriptive titles to give the listener a general idea of scenes, ideas, or events that motivated the music.

Beethoven included a comment at the beginning of the first movement of the *Pastoral* Symphony: "Awakening of cheerful feelings upon arriving in the country." The rest is up to the listener. Beethoven's comments focus your thoughts without a running narration such as, "Here I jumped over a fence; then I chased some birds till I got tired. . . ."

Descriptive Music Plan

There is no general plan for descriptive music since it is incorporated within the other forms. Vivaldi's *The Four Seasons* is a group of solo concertos and follows the concerto plan. Beethoven's *Pastoral* Symphony and Schumann's *Spring* Symphony follow the symphony plan.

Selected Listening

Beethoven	Symphony No. 6 in F Major (*Pastoral*)
Borodin	*In the Steppes of Central Asia*
Brahms	*Academic Festival Overture*
Copland	*Appalachian Spring*
Copland	*El Salón México*
Debussy	*Afternoon of a Faun*
Debussy	*La Mer*
Dvořák	Symphony No. 9 in e minor *(New World)*
Elgar	*Enigma Variations*
Gershwin	*An American in Paris*
Grofé	*Grand Canyon Suite*
Hindemith	*Mathis der Maler*
Holst	*The Planets*
Ives	*Symphony: Holidays*
Mendelssohn	Symphony No. 4 in A Major (*Italian*)
Mussorgsky	*A Night on Bald Mountain*
Rimsky-Korsakov	*Scheherazade*
Schumann	Symphony No. 1 in B-Flat Major (*Spring*)
Stravinsky	*L'Histoire du Soldat (Story of a Soldier)*
Tchaikovsky	*1812 Overture*
Vivaldi	*The Four Seasons*

FORMS USED IN CHURCH AND CHORAL MUSIC

The Mass

Originally part of the Catholic church service, many of these works are performed today as concert works. Masses are often scored for chorus, orchestra, and vocal soloists. Traditionally, the text is in Latin.

Overall Plan of the Mass

The sections of the Mass are fairly standard and come from either the Proper portion (because they are proper for a certain date in the Church calendar) or from the Ordinary section (because they are ordinarily included in every mass). Here are the large sections of the Ordinary Mass:

> **Kyrie** (Lord, have mercy)
>
> **Gloria** (Glory to God in the Highest)
>
> **Credo** (I believe in one God)
>
> **Sanctus** (Holy, Holy, Holy)
>
> **Agnus Dei** (Lamb of God)

In a requiem, a Mass for the dead, the Credo and Gloria sections are omitted, and a section called *Dies irae* ("Day of wrath") is added.

Selected Listening

Bach	Mass in b minor
Beethoven	*Missa Solemnis*
Bernstein	*Mass: A Theater Piece* (nontraditional)
Brahms	*A German Requiem*
Bruckner	Mass in e minor
Haydn	*Mass in Time of War*
Mozart	Mass in C Major (*Coronation*)
Mozart	Mass in c minor
Mozart	*Requiem*
Schubert	Mass in G Major
Verdi	*Requiem*

Oratorio

The oratorio can be described as a religious opera presented as a concert—without the scenery, staging, costumes, or movement of grand opera. Sources of the texts are usually the Old Testament or the New Testament. The oratorio resembles opera in many ways:

- a cast of characters (vocal soloists)

- a chorus, which often represents crowds of people

- an orchestra

- a keyboard accompanist (organ or harpsichord)

- a text in the language of the composer and intended audience, rather than in Church Latin

George Frederic Handel (1685–1759), wrote nineteen oratorios including the famous *Messiah*. Born in Halle, Germany, Handel moved to London where he composed oratorios in English.

Oratorio Plan

Although oratorios differ according to the subject and text, most have many sections featuring narrator, various soloists, soloists in combination, and choruses. Handel's *Messiah* is typical of the Baroque style period oratorio. The outline of its first section follows:

Handel's Messiah (first section)

Overture (orchestra only)

Recitative (narrator, tenor soloist)

Aria (tenor soloist)

Chorus (with orchestra)

Recitative (bass soloist)

Aria (bass soloist)

Selected Listening

Bach	*Christmas Oratorio*
Beethoven	*Christ on the Mount of Olives*
Berlioz	*L'Enfance du Christ (The Childhood of Christ)*
Debussy	*Le Martyre de Saint-Sébastien*
Handel	*Israel in Egypt*
Handel	*Messiah*
Haydn	*The Creation*
Haydn	*The Seasons*
Honegger	*King David*
Mendelssohn	*Elijah*

Cantata

Similar to the oratorio, the cantata is usually shorter and meant to be performed within a church service rather than at a concert. The text is usually from the New Testament, and the Lutheran cantatas incorporate a simple hymnlike tune called a chorale melody.

Martin Luther devised cantatas for his own church services. As a symbol of protest (Protestantism) against the Catholic church, Luther wrote the texts for his cantatas and sermons in German, not Latin, so his congregation could understand them. To further help his congregation relate to the church service, Luther composed many of the chorale melodies with tunes simple enough to be sung and remembered easily.

Composers like Bach wove these chorale melodies throughout sections of the cantata, with the cantata usually ending in a richly harmonized rendition of the chorale melody. While the congregation was leaving the church, Bach often improvised elaborate organ pieces using the chorale melody.

Overall Cantata Plan

Like the oratorio, there is no set plan for cantatas, but all contain contrasting sections featuring various performers. The plan for Bach's Cantata No. 140 (*Wachet auf, "Sleepers awake"*), is typical of the Lutheran cantata:

> **Bach Cantata No. 140 (*Wachet auf, "Sleepers awake"*)**
>
> **Chorus** (chorus and orchestra)
>
> **Recitative** (tenor with accompaniment)
>
> **Aria** (soprano soloist with orchestra)
>
> **Recitative** (alto soloist with accompaniment)
>
> **Duet** (soprano and bass soloists with orchestra)
>
> **Chorus** (chorus and orchestra)

Selected Listening

Bach	Cantata No. 4 *(Christ lag in Todesbanden)*
Bach	Cantata No. 51 *(Jauchzet Gott in allen Landen)*
Bach	Cantata No. 80 *(Ein feste Burg)*
Bach	Cantata No. 140 *(Wachet auf)*

Other Religious Choral Music Forms

In addition to the mass, oratorios, and cantata, a vast body of works exist.

Selected Listening

Bach	*Magnificat in D*
Bach	*Saint Matthew Passion*
Bloch	*Sacred Service (Avodath Hakodesh)*
Britten	*A Ceremony of Carols*
Haydn	*Seven Last Words of Christ*
Stravinsky	*Symphony of Psalms*

FORMS USED IN MUSICAL THEATER

Musical theater includes opera, operetta, and the Broadway Musical. Most musical theater works utilize similar plans in varying order:

> ### *Musical Theater Plans*
>
> - **overture** (orchestra)
> - **arias** (soloist with accompaniment)
> - **recitatives** (speech-like melody, accompanied by keyboard or orchestra)
> - **duets** (song for two soloists with orchestra accompaniment)
> - **trios** (song for three soloists with orchestra accompaniment)
> - **quartets, quintets,** etc. (song for four, five, and more soloists)
> - **choruses** (sections for chorus with orchestra)

Opera

Opera is musical theater at its grandest—rich with drama, dancing, scenery, costumes, vocal soloists, a chorus, and often many supernumeraries (extras) to fill the stage. Based on a story, these productions are accompanied by a symphony orchestra.

Before the stage curtain rises, operas begin with an orchestral **overture.** The remainder of the opera features a variety of musical numbers similar to the other musical theater works as outlined in the above chart.

Selected Listening

Bizet	*Carmen*
Britten	*Peter Grimes*
Gershwin	*Porgy and Bess*
Gounod	*Faust*
Mozart	*Don Giovanni*
Mozart	*The Magic Flute*
Mozart	*The Marriage of Figaro*
Offenbach	*The Tales of Hoffman*
Puccini	*La Bohème*
Puccini	*Madame Butterfly*
Puccini	*Turandot*
Wagner	*Die Meistersinger von Nürnberg*
Verdi	*Rigoletto*
Verdi	*La traviata*
Verdi	*Aida*

Operetta

Operettas have less serious themes than operas and are often called light opera. They have all the trappings of grand opera and may include spoken dialogue.

Selected Listening

Herbert	*Naughty Marietta*
Kalman	*Countess Maritza*
Lehár	*The Merry Widow*
Romberg	*The Desert Song*
Romberg	*The Student Prince*
Strauss	*The Gypsy Baron*
Sullivan	*H.M.S. Pinafore*
Sullivan	*The Mikado*
Sullivan	*The Pirates of Penzance*

Broadway Musical

This popular musical drama centers around a book (story). The musical score often incorporates jazz and popular music styles.

Selected Listening

Leonard Bernstein	*West Side Story* (1957)
Jerry Bock	*Fiddler on the Roof* (1964)
Jerome Kern	*Show Boat* (1927)
Mitch Leigh	*Man of La Mancha* (1965)
Frank Loesser	*Guys and Dolls* (1950)
Frank Loesser	*Most Happy Fella* (1956)
Richard Rodgers	*The Sound of Music*
Claude-Michel Schoenberg	*Les Miserables* (1985)
Claude-Michel Schoenberg	*Miss Saigon* (1990)
Stephen Sondheim	*A Little Night Music* (1973)
Stephen Sondheim	*Sweeney Todd* (1979)
Andrew Lloyd Webber	*Jesus Christ Superstar* (1971)
Andrew Lloyd Webber	*Phantom of the Opera* (1988)

FORMS USED IN BALLET

Ballet is dance theater, often with a story set to music.

Overall Ballet Plan

Ballets are divided into acts and scenes. Similar to musical theater, ballets usually begin with an overture. Then, music for each scene closely follows the story line, for which choreographers devise ballet movement. When a ballet is based on existing music without a story, the form follows the music (suite, rondo, symphony, etc.).

Selected Listening

Copland	*Appalachian Spring*
Copland	*Billy the Kid*
Copland	*Rodeo*
Prokofiev	*Romeo and Juliet*
Stravinsky	*Petrushka*
Tchaikovsky	*The Nutcracker*
Tchaikovsky	*Swan Lake*

FORMS USED IN CHAMBER MUSIC

The vast amount of music for small combinations of instruments is what we refer to as chamber music.

Chamber Music Plans

Chamber music uses forms similar to those in orchestral music. String quartets and string trios by Haydn and Mozart, for example, often use the multimovement form found in symphonies:

> *First Movement*—fast
>
> *Second Movement*—slow
>
> *Third Movement*—moderately fast, dance style
>
> *Fourth Movement*—fast

Selected Listening

Bartók	*Music for Strings, Percussion and Celesta*
Bartók	String Quartets
Beethoven	Sonata for Violin and Piano No. 9 in A Major (*Kreutzer*)
Beethoven	String Quartet Opus 18 No. 1 in F Major

Yo-Yo Ma, cellist (Courtesy of ICM Artists LTD./Photo by Bill King)

Beethoven	String Quartet Opus 18 No. 2 in G Major
Beethoven	String Quartet Opus 18 No. 3 in D Major
Beethoven	String Quartet Opus 18 No. 4 in c minor
Beethoven	String Quartet Opus 18 No. 5 in A Major
Beethoven	String Quartet Opus 18 No. 6 in B-Flat Major
Beethoven	String Quartet Opus 59 No. 1 in F Major
Beethoven	String Quartet Opus 59 No. 2 in e minor
Beethoven	String Quartet Opus 59 No. 3 in C Major
Beethoven	Trio No. 6 in B-Flat (*Archduke*)
Brahms	Clarinet Quintet in b minor
Brahms	Trio in E-Flat for Horn, Violin, and Cello
Debussy	Sonata No. 1 for Cello and Piano
Haydn	String Quartet Opus 76 No. 3 in C Major
Mozart	String Quartet in G Major K. 387
Ravel	String Quartet in F Major
Schubert	Quintet in A Major (*Trout*)
Schumann	Quintet in E-Flat
Stravinsky	Octet for Wind Instruments

FORMS USED IN KEYBOARD MUSIC

Organ

With the construction of the great churches and cathedrals starting in the Middle Ages came the development of large organs. These great instruments could produce music that resounded throughout the huge cavities of the buildings. It was then that a vast literature for the organ was composed. Organists played much of that early music in church concerts or as part of the church service.

Typical pieces for organ before 1750:

chorale preludes	partitas
fugues	toccatas

Harpsichord and Clavichord

Small keyboard instruments, such as harpsichord and clavichord, were popular in the 17th- and 18th-century palaces and homes of the affluent. Typical pieces for these instruments:

suites	partitas
sonatas	fugues

Piano

By the late-18th century, the piano had become the household keyboard instrument. Mozart added to its popularity by composing sonatas and concertos, performing these piano works himself at concerts throughout the great courts of Europe. Building on the Mozart works, Beethoven's powerful sonatas and concertos for piano and an enlarged orchestra added new, dramatic dimension to the literature.

Coinciding with the expanding popularity of the piano during the nineteenth century was the growth of printed, published music. The strong sales of piano music encouraged composers such as Beethoven, Chopin, Schumann, Brahms, and many others to write music for the piano. By the mid-nineteenthth century, the ten to twenty-minute sonata was largely replaced by new shorter forms, most lasting from a minute-and-a-half to six minutes.

ballades	polonaises
consolations	preludes
études	rhapsodies
fantasies	songs without words
impromptus	waltzes
mazurkas	

Keyboard Music Plans

The Baroque suite for harpsichord is identical to the chamber ensemble and orchestral suite: it is a group of dance-style pieces.

The Baroque keyboard sonata is fairly free form, usually "free-sectional." The term *sonata* comes from the Latin *sonare,* which means "to sound." It was used in Baroque instrumental pieces to distinguish them from pieces to be sung, from *cantatas, cantare.*

Electronic synthesizers and keyboards have brought about a renewed interest in keyboards in recent years. The new instruments can reproduce

Vladimir Ashkenazy, pianist (Courtesy of ICM Artists LTD.)

music of the past with the variety of tone qualities—harpsichord, piano, electric piano, strings, brass, etc. The synthesizer also enables the performer to create new sounds.

Selected Listening

Bach	*The Art of Fugue*
Bach	Organ Preludes and Fugues
Beethoven	Sonata No. 8 in c minor (*Pathétique)*
Beethoven	Sonata No. 14 in c-sharp minor (*Moonlight*)
Carlos	*Episodes for Piano and Electronic Sound*
Chopin	Ballades 1–4
Chopin	Études (Opus 10 and 25)
Chopin	Mazurkas
Chopin	Nocturnes
Chopin	Preludes
Liszt	Consolations
Liszt	*Fantasia and Fugue on BACH* (organ solo)
Liszt	*Hungarian* Rhapsodies
Mendelssohn	Preludes and Fugues for Piano
Mendelssohn	*Songs Without Words* (Opus 38, 62, 67)
Mozart	Piano Sonatas
Scarlatti	Harpsichord Sonatas
Schumann	*Carnaval*
Schumann	*Papillons*

WHAT IS THE ROLE OF FORM IN MUSIC?

Most music has a unified structure, order, or **form** to assist listeners in its understanding. Composers introduce musical ideas and develop them. The idea can be a short melodic or rhythmic fragment we call a **motive.** Or, the idea can be a longer unit such as a melody. Unification of form comes when these musical ideas are reintroduced—exactly or with some modification.

As in literature or in theater, it is difficult to make sense of a work when an author or composer rambles, introducing one new idea after another without developing or repeating any of them. In a play, for instance, characters are introduced. As the play progresses, we get to know each character in greater depth. We still recognize that character, even with changes of costume or make-up. We would feel lost if new characters continually appeared and disappeared without being developed or ever reappearing.

In music, melodies and melodic fragments are modified as they are played by different instruments or by slight changes in the pitch of the idea. Those changes can be compared to costume and make-up changes. The point is that we enjoy getting to know the musical ideas and hearing them go through modifications.

WHAT DETAILED FORMS ARE USED IN CLASSICAL MUSIC?

We have discussed the large multi-movement forms such as symphonies, concertos, cantatas, etc. The movements are like the outer structure of a large building. Within each movement, composers organize their music in more detailed forms, much like the detailed infrastructure of a building: floors, rooms, hallways. The Detailed Forms chart on page 101 presents an overview of the typical detailed forms composers use to unify their works. The letters refer to the different melodies or themes. For instance, **A** would be the first and usually the main theme of the movement or section. **B** refers to the second melody or theme, etc.

STROPHIC SONG FORM

You know this form. It is commonly used in popular songs, church hymns, folk songs, and patriotic songs. The melody is repeated a number of times, each time with new words. "Tom Dooley" (page 102) is a good example of the strophic form.

A	main melody
A^1	same melody with a different text
A^2	same melody with yet another text

DETAILED FORMS

Form	Sections	Typical Uses
Strophic	A A^2 A^3 etc.	Songs (music repeated with new lyrics)
Through-composed	A B C D E F etc.	Songs, instrumental music (music keeps changing)
Free sectional	A B A B C or A B C B or A B C A D B C , etc.	Instrumental music (some sections may repeat)
Two-part	A B , or A A B B	Songs, movements of large works
Three-part	A B A	Songs, arias, movements of large works
Rondo	A B A C A or A B A C A B A or A B A C A D A	Last movement of concerto, symphony movements, chamber music, sonata

Song-Form with Trio Form

	Sections	Typical Uses
Minuet/scherzo	A A B B A	Dance movements of symphonies, string quartets
Trio	C C D C C D C	
Minuet	A A B B A	

Form	Sections	Typical Uses
Theme and variations	A A^1 A^2 A^3 A^4 etc. theme + var^1 + var^2, etc.	movement in symphony, chamber music, sonata

Sonata

Exposition

A A B C usually repeat to beginning
(optional)

Development

A, **B**, or **C** themes manipulated

Recapitulation

A A B C
(optional)

Coda

Typical Uses: movement in symphony, chamber music, sonata, concerto

Tom Dooley

THROUGH-COMPOSED FORM

The melody keeps changing and rarely repeats. Many instrumental works, art songs, and dramatic works portraying stories use a through-composed form.

A   first melody

B   second and different melody

| C | third and different melody |
| D | fourth and different melody |

Through-Composed Form: Selected Listening

Berlioz	*Symphonie fantastique* [5th movement]
Schubert	*The Erlking (Erlkönig) (art song)*
Strauss, R.	*Till Eulenspiegel's Merry Pranks*
	(Till Eulenspiegels lustige Streiche)
Tchaikovsky	*1812 Overture*

FREE-SECTIONAL FORM

This form is similar to the through-composed song, except the main sections of the music are sometimes repeated. It was a popular form in the Baroque period.

‖: **A** :‖	(: = repeat section)
‖: **B** :‖	second melody
‖: **C** :‖	third and different melody
‖: **D** :‖	fourth and different melody

Free Sectional Form: Selected Listening

Corelli	Concerti Grossi Opus 6
Gabrieli	*Sonata pian'e forte*
Gabrieli	*Symphoniae sacrae*
Stravinsky	*Petrushka*
Vivaldi	*The Four Seasons*

TWO-PART FORM (BINARY)

There are two different sections of melody, or on a large scale, two different melodies. The patriotic song "America" is in binary form.

| A | B |

Vienna Choir Boys (Courtesy of ICM Artists LTD.)

Section A

My country 'tis of thee,
Sweet land of liberty,
Of thee I sing.

Section B

Land where my fathers died,
Land of the pilgrim's pride
From every mountain side,
Let freedom ring.

Two-Part Form: Selected Listening

Bernstein	*Seven Anniversaries* No. 2
Brahms	Waltzes Opus 39 Nos. 5 and 6
Chopin	Mazurkas Nos. 7, 11, 14, 26
Mendelssohn	*Song Without Words* No. 6
Schumann	*Kinderszenen* Opus 15 No. 10

THREE-PART FORM (TERNARY)

You know this form well. Most popular songs use it—it's one of the most common in all of music. The typical popular song has a main melody (A), which becomes familiar, followed by a contrasting middle section (B), often forgettable, and a return to the main melody (A). The song "Deck the Halls" (page 105) uses a three-part (ternary) form.

Deck the Halls

| **A** main melody | **B** contrasting melody | **A** repeat of the main melody |

Here are some popular songs which use this three-part form:

Leigh	"The Impossible Dream"
Gershwin	"A Foggy Day"
Gershwin	"I Got Rhythm"
Lennon/McCartney	"Yesterday"
Wilson	"Seventy-Six Trombones"

Large sections of longer works often use the three-part form, for example, arias in operas, oratorios, and cantatas. Like the popular song, the middle section of an aria has a contrasting style. If we look at form more broadly, we can also view the sonata form and the minuet and trio form as ternary forms. They each contain a main section (A), a contrasting section (B), and a return to the ideas of the main section (A).

The second movement of Beethoven's Symphony No. 3 (*Eroica*) is constructed in three sections:

| **A** *funeral march* in minor tonality | **B** *contrasting section* in major tonality | **A** *funeral march* in minor tonality |

Three-Part Form: Selected Listening

Bach	Cantata No. 140 (tenor aria)
Handel	*Messiah* (soprano and alto arias)
Mendelssohn	*Songs Without Words* Nos. 1, 22, and 44

RONDO FORM

The main ingredient in rondo form is a constantly returning main melody, alternating with less important melodies. The form could be charted in the following ways:

(A = main theme or melody; B, C, D, etc. = other themes)

A	B	A	C	A

or

A	B	A	C	A	B	A

or

A	B	A	C	A	D	A

The last movement of concertos and sonatas often uses the rondo form. You will hear the main melody over and over. A typical rondo in a Mozart piano concerto is fast, happy, and witty, with a catchy, identifiable melody.

Rondo Form: Selected Listening

Beethoven	Piano Concerto No. 1 in C Major [3rd movement]
Beethoven	Piano Concerto No. 2 in B-Flat Major [3rd movement]
Beethoven	Piano Concerto No. 3 in c minor [3rd movement]
Beethoven	Piano Concerto No. 4 in G Major [3rd movement]
Beethoven	Piano Concerto No. 5 in E-Flat Major (*Emperor*) [3rd movement]
Beethoven	Piano Sonata No. 8 in c minor (*Pathétique*) [3rd movement]
Beethoven	Violin Concerto in D Major [3rd movement]
Brahms	Violin Concerto in D Major [3rd movement]
Debussy	*Images*
Mozart	Piano Concerto No. 15 in B-Flat Major [3rd movement]
Mozart	Piano Concerto No. 23 in A Major [3rd movement]
Prokofiev	Symphony No. 5 [4th movement]

SONG-FORM WITH TRIO FORM

Both the minuet-and-trio and the scherzo-and-trio use this form. During the 18th century, the popularity of the court dance (the minuet) was at its peak. As a result, the happy, graceful style of this 3/4-time dance was incorporated into symphonies and chamber music works, and occasionally into piano sonatas. Audiences loved to hear it at concerts as well as at court dances.

Lighter in character, the trio calls for fewer instruments. It got its name from the Baroque trio sonata, which uses only three instruments. The trio section follows the minuet without a pause. When it concludes, the music returns to the minuet section.

The overall form has three parts, A–B–A: the minuet section (A), the trio section (B), and the repeat of the minuet section (A). Within this large form, the Song-Form with Trio Form incorporates short sections that are repeated. The form could be charted as follows:

Song-Form with Trio Form (Minuet/Scherzo with Trio Form)

Minuet Section (A)

Theme A	**Theme A** – modified

both sections repeat

Theme B	**Theme A** – modified

both sections repeat

Trio Section (B)

Theme C	**Theme C** – modified

both sections repeat

Theme D	**Theme C** – modified

both sections repeat

Minuet Section (A) (same as beginning)

Theme A	**Theme A** – modified

usually no repeats

Theme B	**Theme A** – modified

usually no repeats

Song-Form with Trio Form: Selected Listening

Beethoven	Symphony No. 2 in D Major [3rd movement]
Beethoven	Symphony No. 3 in E-Flat (*Eroica*) [3rd movement]
Beethoven	Symphony No. 5 in c minor [3rd movement]

Beethoven	Symphony No. 6 in F Major (*Pastoral*) [3rd movement]
Berlioz	*Symphonie fantastique* [2nd, 3rd, and 4th movements]
Brahms	Symphony No. 1 in c minor [2nd movement]
Brahms	Symphony No. 3 in F Major [3rd movement]
Haydn	String Quartets [3rd movements]
Haydn	Symphony No. 88 in G Major [3rd movement]
Haydn	Symphony No. 94 in G Major (*Surprise*) [3rd movement]
Haydn	Symphony No. 101 in D Major (*Clock*) [3rd movement]
Haydn	Symphony No. 104 in D Major (*London*) [3rd movement]
Mozart	Symphony No. 35 in D Major (*Haffner*) [3rd movement]
Mozart	Symphony No. 39 in E-Flat [3rd movement]
Mozart	Symphony No. 40 in g minor [3rd movement]
Mozart	Symphony No. 41 in C Major (*Jupiter*) [3rd movement]
Prokofiev	Piano Concerto No. 2 in g minor [2nd movement]

THEME AND VARIATIONS

A main theme stated at the beginning recurs with slight changes in each subsequent section. Although usually still recognizable, the theme goes through a series of variations or transformations. The variations may include changes from major to minor, added counter melodies, changes of texture, and changes of orchestration. The form could be charted as follows:

A main theme	**A**^{1} variation 1	**A**^{2} variation 2	**A**^{3} variation 3	**A**^{4} variation 4

Composers from all style periods have delighted their audiences with inventive variations. They used this form in sections of symphonies, chamber music, sonatas, and even vocal music, ballet, and opera.

Theme and Variations: Selected Listening

Beethoven	Symphony No. 9 in d minor (*Choral*) [4th movement]
Brahms	Symphony No. 4 in e minor [4th movement]
Brahms	*Variations on a Theme by Haydn*
Britten	*The Young Person's Guide to the Orchestra*
Haydn	Symphony No. 94 in G Major (*Surprise*) [2nd movement]
Mozart	Variations, *Ah, vous dirai-je, maman (Twinkle, Twinkle, Little Star)*
Schoenberg	*Variations for Orchestra*
Stravinsky	Octet for Wind Instruments [2nd movement]

SONATA FORM

You'll hear the sonata form in the first movements of Classical period symphonies, concertos, sonatas, and string quartets. The form was so popular in the Classical period that Mozart, Haydn, and Beethoven often used it in two or three movements of a four-movement work.

The main concept in sonata-allegro form is theme and development. The *exposition,* with two or three main themes, opens the movement. The entire exposition is usually repeated. The next section, the *development,* uses themes in a fanciful way, incorporating imitation, sequences, changes of tonality, and orchestration. In the *recapitulation,* the music returns to the main themes, and the *coda* brings the movement to a conclusion. A chart of the sonata form is presented in Figure 3-1.

WHAT MUSICAL STYLES AM I LIKELY TO HEAR AT CONCERTS?

Most of the music you will hear at concerts is from four main periods:

Baroque (1600–1750)

Classical (1750–1820)

Romantic (1820–1900)

20th-century (1900 to the present)

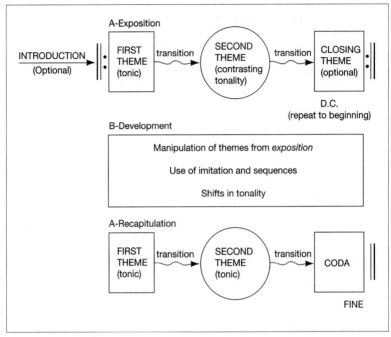

Figure 3-1   Sonata Form

Once familiar with the style period, you can predict what the music will be like. After a while, you will be able to identify the style period of a piece the first time you hear it.

If you're familiar with the characteristics of the Classical period and have listened to some of Mozart's music, you will have a good idea what Haydn's music will sound like. And when you hear a new piece of music from that period, you will probably be able to guess the composer or at least think of a composer of the same period who might have written it.

The charts on the following pages are handy overviews of the major musical style periods. Use them as guidelines in your listening. If you memorize them, you will be a more informed listener at concerts.

THE BAROQUE PERIOD (1600–1750)

IMPORTANT COMPOSERS

Giovanni Gabrieli, Claudio Monteverdi, Heinrich Schütz, Jean-Baptiste Lully, Archangelo Corelli, Henry Purcell, Alessandro Scarlatti, Domenico Scarlatti, Jean-Philippe Rameau, Antonio Vivaldi, Johann Sebastian Bach, George Frideric Handel

ARTISTS

Gianlorenzo Bernini, Caravaggio, El Greco, Frans Hals, Rembrandt van Rijn, Peter Paul Rubens, Anthony Van Dyke

WRITERS

John Donne, John Milton, Alexander Pope, William Shakespeare, Jonathan Swift

PHILOSOPHERS

Francis Bacon, Rene Descartes, Thomas Hobbes, Matthew Locke, Baruch Spinoza

SOCIAL, POLITICAL, AND CULTURAL EVENTS

First opera (c. 1600), Shakespeare's *Hamlet* (1600), King James version of the *Bible* (1611), Pilgrims land in America (1620), first opera house (1637), reign of Louis XIV (1643–1715), Newton's physical laws, beginning of Age of Enlightenment, expansion of Colonialism

CHARACTERISTICS OF BAROQUE MUSIC

GENERAL

Music often heavy, grand, and expansive; often includes both singers and instruments

PERFORMING MEDIA

Chamber orchestra, chorus and chamber orchestra, soloist(s) and chamber orchestra, chamber ensemble, organ, harpsichord

RHYTHM

Steady beats, running bass, complicated driving rhythms; meters: 2, 3, 4, 6; slowing down to end the piece

MELODY

Major and minor melodies; sequence, imitation, and elaborate ornamentation

HARMONY

Strong harmonic movement; harmonic sequences and recurring cadences; major and minor tonalities

EXPRESSION

Layered dynamics, echo imitation used; loud and soft juxtaposed—no crescendo or diminuendo

TEXTURE

Mainly polyphonic, thick texture; one or more melodies in high parts with countermelodies; harmonic fill parts and continuous bass line; occasional homophony (sounding together)

FORMS

Concerto, concerto grosso, suite, oratorio, cantata, opera, trio sonata and other sonatas for instruments, keyboard prelude, fugue, toccata

THE CLASSICAL PERIOD (1750–1820)

IMPORTANT COMPOSERS

Joseph Haydn, Wolfgang Amadeus Mozart, Ludwig van Beethoven (early works)

WRITERS

Robert Burns, Johann Wolfgang Goethe, Thomas Jefferson, Samuel Johnson, Alexander Pope, Johann Schiller

ARTISTS

Jacques-Louis David, Jean-August Ingres

PHILOSOPHERS

Denis Diderot, David Hume, Immanuel Kant, Jean-Jacques Rousseau, Voltaire (Francois-Marie Arouet)

SOCIAL, POLITICAL, AND CULTURAL EVENTS

Factory system begins in England; James Watt's steam engine; American and French Revolution; Napoleon in power; Catherine the Great of Russia; Hapsburgs rule Austria, Hungary, Italy, Spain, and the Netherlands; The American Constitution, the Age of Reason

CHARACTERISTICS OF CLASSICAL MUSIC

GENERAL

Elegant, restrained, stable, balanced; predictable, with clear musical ideas: you seem to know the music even on the first hearing

PERFORMING MEDIUM

Symphony orchestra, chamber orchestra, soloists and orchestra, piano, chamber ensembles, opera companies

RHYTHM

Simple, regular rhythms with steady beat; steady tempos with little change; meters mostly 2, 3, 4, 6

MELODY

Lightly ornamented melodies; running scale patterns and broken chords; imitation and sequences, symmetrical phrases

HARMONY

Chords by thirds, mostly built on scale tones; strong tonal center (key); major and minor tonalities

EXPRESSION

Moderate use of crescendo, diminuendo; neither very soft nor very loud (mostly *p, mf, f*)

TEXTURE

Basically homophonic—melody (usually on top) with chordal accompaniment; some polyphony, mainly in development sections; polyphony is less formal than in Baroque era; textures change frequently

FORMS

Clear-cut, easy to follow; sections set off by obvious cadences and stops; exact repetition of sections; detailed forms: two-part and three-part forms; sonata, rondo, minuet and trio, theme and variations; large forms: symphony, concerto, sonata, string trio and quartet; opera; some oratorios and masses

THE ROMANTIC PERIOD (1820–1900)

IMPORTANT COMPOSERS

Ludwig van Beethoven, Hector Berlioz, Georges Bizet, Alexander Borodin, Johannes Brahms, Anton Bruckner, Frederic Chopin, Claude Debussy, Henri Duparc, Anton Dvořák, Edward Elgar, Gabriel Fauré, Mikhail Glinka, Charles Gounod, Edvard Grieg, Franz Liszt, Gustav Mahler, Felix Mendelssohn, Modest Mussorgsky, Jacques Offenbach, Giacomo Puccini, Nikolai Rimsky-Korsakov, Camille Saint-Saëns, Franz Schubert, Robert Schumann, Jan Sibelius, Bedrich Smetana, Johann Strauss Jr. & Sr., Richard Strauss, Peter Tchaikovsky, Giuseppi Verdi, Carl Maria von Weber, Richard Wagner

ARTISTS

William Blake, Paul Cézanne, Honoré Daumier, Edgar Dégas, Eugene Delacroix, Paul Gauguin, Francisco Goya, Claude Monet, Pierre-August Renoir, August Rodin, Georges Seurat, Joseph Turner, Vincent van Gogh

WRITERS

Honoré de Balzac, Robert Browning, George Gordon Lord Byron, Anton Chekhov, Samuel Coleridge, Charles Dickens, Emily Dickinson, Fyodor Dostoevski, Nathaniel Hawthorne, Heinrich Heine, Victor Hugo, Henrik Ibsen, Henry James, John Keats, Henry Wadsworth Longfellow, Edgar Allan Poe, Aleksandr Pushkin, George Sand, Percy Bysshe Shelley, Marie-Henri Stendhal, Robert Louis Stevenson, Harriet Beecher Stowe, Alfred Lord Tennyson, William Thackeray, Leo Tolstoy, Mark Twain, Walt Whitman, Oscar Wilde, William Wordsworth

PHILOSOPHERS

August Comte, Ralph Waldo Emerson, Friedrich Engels, Ernest Haeckel, Georg Hegel, Thomas Henry Huxley, Søren Kierkegaard, Karl Marx, John Stuart Mill, Friedrich Nietzsche, Arthur Schopenhauer, Herbert Spencer, Henry David Thoreau

SOCIAL, POLITICAL, AND CULTURAL EVENTS

Industrial Revolution, steamboat, railroads, photography, telegraph, telephone, phonograph, Monroe Doctrine, California Gold Rush, unification of Germany and Italy, reign of Victoria, "Gay 90s," Darwin's *The Descent of Man,* American War Between the States

CHARACTERISTICS OF ROMANTIC MUSIC

GENERAL

Music has an emotional, subjective quality with frequent mood changes; expansive sound with large ensembles; intimate music with small ensembles; literature or extra-musical ideas often serve as basis for the music

PERFORMING MEDIA

Large symphony orchestras, piano, chamber music ensembles, opera and ballet companies

RHYTHM

Rubato used often; changing tempos within sections and movements; more complex rhythms than in previous periods

MELODY

Long, flowing, emotion-laden melodies; also short themes representing ideas or people; major and minor melodies with chromatic alterations; instrumental melodies with wide leaps and range

HARMONY

Tonal (key-centered), but with increasing use of modulations and chromatic tones; rich, complex harmonies

EXPRESSION

Full range of dynamics (extremely soft to extremely loud); extensive use of crescendo and diminuendo

TEXTURE

Mainly homophonic (melody with accompaniment); occasional use of polyphony

FORMS

Some continued use of Classical period forms; symphony, often with titles; concerto; new, small piano forms (nocturne, ballade, etude, waltz, mazurka); opera, ballet, symphonic tone poem, concert overture; programmatic and descriptive works.

THE TWENTIETH CENTURY PERIOD (1900 TO THE PRESENT)

IMPORTANT COMPOSERS

Samuel Barber, Béla Bartók, Alban Berg, Leonard Bernstein, Ernst Bloch, Pierre Boulez, Benjamin Britten, Aaron Copland, Edward Elgar, Manuel de Falla, Gabriel Fauré, George Gershwin, Edvard Grieg, Paul Hindemith, Gustav Holst, Arthur Honegger, Charles Ives, Leoš Janáček, Jerome Kern, Zoltán Kodály, Franz Lehar, Oliver Messiaen, Gian Carlo Menotti, Darius Milhaud, Francis Poulenc, Sergei Prokofiev, Sergei Rachmaninoff, Maurice Ravel, Ottorino Respighi, Richard Rodgers, Sigmund Romberg, Arnold Schoenberg, William Schuman, Alexander Scriabin, Dmitri Shostakovich, Jan Sibelius, Karlheinz Stockhausen, Richard Strauss, Igor Stravinsky, Edgar Varèse, William Walton, Kurt Weill, Ralph Vaughan Williams, Anton Webern

VISUAL ARTISTS

Max Beckmann, Georges Braque, Alexander Calder, Marc Chagall, Salvador Dali, Willem De Kooning, Walt Disney, Marcel Duchamp, Max Ernst, Buckminster Fuller, Juan Gris, Wassily Kandinsky, Paul Klee, Le Corbusier, Henri Matisse, Mies van der Rohe, Joan Miró, Amedeo Modigliani, Piet Mondrian, Claude Monet, Henry Moore, Georgia O'Keeffe, Pablo Picasso, Jackson Pollock, Auguste Renoir, August Rodin, Georges Rouault, Henri Rousseau, Eero Saarinen, Maurice Utrillo, Andy Warhol, Frank Lloyd Wright, Andrew Wyeth

WRITERS

Edward Albee, Bertold Brecht, Truman Capote, Joseph Conrad, e. e. cummings, T. S. Eliot, William Faulkner, F. Scott Fitzgerald, Robert Frost, Ernest Hemingway, Aldous Huxley, A. E. Houseman, Henrik Ibsen, Henry James, James Joyce, Franz Kafka, Norman Mailer, Thomas Mann, Arthur Miller, O. Henry, Eugene O'Neill, Carl Sandburg, George Bernard Shaw, Neil Simon, John Steinbeck, August Strindberg, Leo Tolstoi, Mark Twain, H. G. Wells, Tennessee Williams, Thomas Wolfe

PHILOSOPHERS

Alfred Adler, Martin Buber, Teilhard de Chardin, John Dewey, Sigmund Freud, Eric Fromm, Mahatma Gandhi, Carl Jung, Martin Luther King, Jr., Mao Tse-tung, Bertrand Russell, George Santayana, Jean-Paul Sartre

SOCIAL, POLITICAL, AND CULTURAL EVENTS

Freud's psychoanalytic theories, jazz, Einstein's relativity theories, United Nations, World Wars I & II, Russian Revolution, Great Depression—U.S. and Europe, Korean War, Vietnam War, Common Market (European Economic Community), Pop art, Op art, chance music and painting, dadaism

SCIENCE, TECHNOLOGY

Ford's production-line automobile, telephone, airplane, computer, films, television, phonograph, microchip, semiconductor, laser technology, penicillin, smallpox vaccine, polio vaccine, "Sputnik," man on the moon, organ transplantation

CHARACTERISTICS OF TWENTIETH CENTURY MUSIC

GENERAL

Music often sounds dissonant, complex, asymmetrical, emotional, objective, satirical; often experimental, eclectic resources

PERFORMING MEDIA

Chamber orchestra and ensembles used more often than symphony orchestra; all previous media still used; electronic synthesizers and keyboards; mixed media: pre-recorded electronic sounds combined with traditional instruments; computer-generated sounds

RHYTHM

Polyrhythms (layers of different rhythms), polymeters, irregular rhythmic patterns, ostinato (recurring patterns)

MELODY

Wide ranges of voices and instruments; fragmented, disjunct, exotic intervals and scales (Asian, chromatic, pentatonic, whole-tone, twelve-tone, quarter-tone)

HARMONY

Extensive use of dissonance; polychords (two or more different chords together), clusters (chords by seconds), quartal harmony (chords by fourths); exotic, experimental sounds

EXPRESSION

All previous techniques still used; extreme effects, including silence

TEXTURE

Polyphonic texture often used; mixes of polyphonic and homophonic; layers of ideas and sounds

FORMS

All forms of the previous periods used, but highly modified; experimental forms

> *Music Concrete:* traditional and environmental sounds manipulated on the tape recorder

> *Chance Music:* also called aleatory—improvised, unpredictable, vague or non-specific notation

> *Electronic Music:* electronically produced sounds, also called synthesizer music

> *Computer Music:* electronic music organized and manipulated by the computer

James Galway, flutist (Courtesy of ICM Artists Ltd.)

4

WHAT TO LISTEN FOR IN THE MUSIC

Music, like all the arts, can accommodate all viewpoints. Each of us perceives differently. How you listen is up to you. There are no restrictions, no single or correct way to listen *to* music.

I will, however, suggest many things you can listen *for* in the music. The opportunity to heighten your experience is boundless.

LEVELS OF LISTENING

THE SENSORY LEVEL

Some listeners enjoy a sound bath, letting music merely wash over them. This passive rather than active listening can be relaxing, like basking on a beach on a sunny day with the surf rushing back and forth over you. Since it takes no effort and feels great, you can allow your brain to idle in neutral and your spine to tingle.

THE EMOTIONAL LEVEL

Music often speaks directly to our emotions. If you have ever listened to music and found yourself daydreaming or reminiscing, your emotions become part of the listening experience. There, in your private world, that

Lynn Harrell, cellist (Courtesy of Lynn Harrell)

beautiful melody by Chopin stirs your deepest feelings—the ones that rarely rise to the surface, the feelings you might not verbalize.

THE SCRIPT LEVEL

Most music has no story associated with it. But if you find yourself making up a story or unraveling a plot while listening to the music, you may be listening at the script level.

THE AWARE LEVEL

Great music has layers of subtleties that invite your awareness, and that is where the excitement begins. You may still enjoy the sensory and emotional effects of the music, but you listen with a new insight and involvement.

REACHING THE AWARE LEVEL

The good news is that you do not have to be a trained musician to reach this level. You can develop the ability to focus on the music itself without any extramusical guidance, pictures, or stories. You can understand and experience the composer's creative choices in the music itself.

When you achieve this awareness, you can follow the musical lines and patterns that the sounds create. You'll notice which instruments are performing, the type of ornamentation in the melody, the texture or stacking of parts, and the harmony. You will recognize which forms the composer used to organize the music. You can discern the performer's tone quality, phrasing, consistency of style, and faithfulness to the composer's intentions.

MUSIC LISTENING GUIDE

Use the listening guide on page 124 to help you reach the aware level. Start by focusing on each element of musical materials. Not every item occurs in every composition, but the guide gives you a checklist of the possibilities. As you listen to a piece of music, the guide can help you discover and appreciate the composer's creative choices.

Phillippe Entremont, pianist (Courtesy of ICM Artists LTD./Photo by Eleanor Morrison)

MUSIC LISTENING GUIDE

PERFORMING MEDIUM

symphony orchestra
chamber orchestra
wind ensemble (band)
chamber music ensemble
electronic instruments

chorus (a cappella)
chorus with orchestra
solo (instrumental or vocal
    with orchestra)
solo (instrumental or vocal
    with piano)
other combinations

RHYTHM-TEMPO-METER

beat prominence: strong,
    weak
tempo: slow, medium, fast
meter: 2, 3, other (5, 7, etc.)
subdivision: simple (2 or 4)
    complex (3, 5, 7, 9)

rubato (changing)
ostinato (repetitous)
basso continuo (running
    bass line)
syncopation
silence

MELODY

prominent
not prominent
smooth (long lines)
fragmented (short lines)
ornamented (trills, etc.)
plain (no ornaments)
imitation (repeated idea, in
    another voice or
    instrument)

sequences (repeated idea,
    same voice, new pitches)
traditional scales used:
    major, minor
other scales used:
    chromatic, pentatonic,
    whole tone, tone-row,
    gapped

HARMONY–TONALITY

mostly consonant (pleasant)
mostly dissonant (unpleasant)
major and minor chords
    (traditional)
polychords

quartal chords (fourths)
clusters (seconds)
major or minor tonality
polytonality
atonality

TEXTURE

monophonic (single line)
polyphonic (many independent lines)
homophonic (sounding together; also melody with
   accompaniment)
mixture of textures

FORM

large forms	*detailed forms*
symphony	strophic (A–A–A, etc.)
concerto	through-composed
concerto grosso	free sectional
opera overture	two-part (A–B, or
concert overture	A–A–B–B)
orchestral suite	three-part (A–B–A)
descriptive piece	rondo (A-B-A-C-A, etc.)
mass	minuet and trio
oratorio	theme and variations
cantata	sonata
opera	
chamber music	*general concept of form*
(trio, quartet, quintet,	developmental
sonata)	(repetition of ideas)
keyboard forms	through-composed
(sonata, fugue, nocturne,	(rhapsodic, little
etc.)	repetition)

EXPLANATION OF THE GUIDE

PERFORMING MEDIUM

It doesn't take an expert to distinguish between a symphony orchestra and
a string quartet. With experience you will also be able to recognize and
identify the sounds of the individual instruments and singing voices. If you
want to review the types of performing groups and suggested listening,
you will find the information in Chapter 1.

Pinchas Zuckerman, violinist (Courtesy of ICM Artists LTD./photo by Christian Steiner)

RHYTHM-TEMPO-METER

Beat Prominence

One of the most easily perceived elements in music is the beat or the lack of it. Even babies and animals respond to a thumping beat. Once in a while, a beat is so vague you will have trouble finding or responding to it; instead, the music has a floating feeling to it. Debussy's Nocturnes and *Afternoon of a Faun* are good examples.

Contrast that with the strong beat in ballet, march, and popular music—for example, Aaron Copland's "Buckaroo Holiday" from his ballet *Rodeo.*

Tempo

The tempo is the speed of the music. You can measure it easily, the same way you measure your pulse beat. Using the second hand of a clock or a timer, count the beats in fifteen seconds of music. Multiply this number by four and you will have the number of beats per minute.

Our perception of tempo seems to correspond to our own pulse rate. We perceive a tempo as being moderate (*moderato* in Italian) when it is close to our own pulse, usually between seventy-two and eighty-six beats per minute. An example of moderato is the "Blues" section from Gershwin's *An American in Paris*.

A slow tempo is perceived as slower than our own heartbeat, usually below seventy-two beats per minute. Listen to the second movement of Beethoven's Piano Concerto No. 5 (*Emperor*), a tempo of about forty beats per minute. Fast tempos are eighty-six beats per minute or faster. Listen to "Hoe Down" from Copland's ballet *Rodeo*.

Italian Tempo Terms

Among the Italians' many contributions to music are tempo markings. Musicians use these terms to describe the character and speed of the music. You will find them in printed concert programs and on record jackets.

Italian Tempo Terms (from slow to fast)	
grave	(extremely slow and solemn)
largo	(very slow, broadly)
lento	(slow)
adagio	(slow, leisurely)
andante	(slow to moderate walking pace)
moderato	(moderate)
allegretto	(moderately fast)
allegro	(fast, lively)
vivace	(very fast)
presto	(very fast)
prestissimo	(as fast as possible)

Tempo Changes

Tempos within sections of concert music may also change. The first movement of Haydn's Symphony No. 94 (*Surprise*) starts with a one-minute *adagio* introduction, then shifts to an *allegro* tempo for the rest of the movement. The shift is not the surprise, by the way. That comes in the second movement with a very loud chord at the end of a quiet section—Haydn's joke to wake up the daydreamers.

Besides sudden shifts in tempo, some music becomes gradually faster (*accelerando*) as in the last movement of Bela Bartok's *Concerto for Orchestra,* or gradually slower (*rallentando*) as in the opening section of Copland's *El salón México.* To bring out the dramatic qualities of the music, performers occasionally deviate slightly from the steady tempo by rushing and then slowing. This effect in music is called *rubato.* Listen to any performance of Chopin's piano music and you'll hear it.

Meter

Meter refers to the regular grouping or pattern of beats. The ones you hear most frequently are four, three, and two, in that order. So often is the four meter used that musicians call it common time. March-style music has meters of two or four. Waltzes and minuets are usually in a three meter. This is discussed in Chapter 2, pp. 00. You may want to review the listening suggestions in that section to become acquainted with the typical meters.

Subdivision of Beats

Rhythm patterns superimposed over the basic beat further subdivide the beat into interesting groupings. Simple subdivisions are multiples of two. All other subdivisions (threes, fives, sevens, etc.) are considered complex or compound. Examples of simple subdivision are the rhythms of the opening melodies in the second movement of Haydn's Symphony No. 94 and in the second movement of Beethoven's Symphony No. 7. A clear example of compound subdivision is evident throughout the last movement of Beethoven's Violin Concerto.

Ostinato

Twentieth-century composers often use a repetitive, rhythmic pattern called *ostinato.* Jazz, rock, and dance music depend heavily on the rhythmic ostinato—the driving rhythm that dancers enjoy. In his thirteen-minute orchestral work *Bolero,* Ravel uses the Spanish bolero rhythm from beginning to end. Over the rhythmic ostinato, Ravel scored a constantly changing instrumentation. He wanted to achieve a long, gradual, crescendo effect. It works!

Basso Continuo

You are familiar with the running bass line in boogie-woogie, swing, or rock music. You will also find it in most Baroque music, such as the first movements of Bach's Brandenburg Concertos Nos. 2 and 5. The bass line provides not only a harmonic foundation but also an interesting rhythmic line.

Silence

Yes, silence is also a part of music. The absence of sound can create very dramatic rhythmic effects. The opening of Mozart's Symphony No. 35 has moments of silence that dramatically introduce the main theme. The first section of Wagner's "Prelude and Love-Death" from *Tristan and Isolde* has many moments of silence which help to portray the anguish of the separated lovers.

4'33" by John Cage is made up entirely of silence. To "perform" this work, the player comes out on stage, sits at the piano, and starts a stop watch. After waiting in silence for exactly four minutes and thirty-three seconds, the performer rises and exits, leaving it up to each member of the audience to fill that silence with his or her own musical imagination.

MELODY

Prominence of Melody

Can you follow a melody, or is it so hidden that you can't find it? Most concert music has a prominent melody. Leonard Bernstein calls melody "the meat and potatoes of music." However, some twentieth-century composers experimented by creating music without recognizable melody. In Penderecki's *Polymorphia* you would be hard pressed to find one—certainly there is no melody you could whistle or hum.

Length of Phrase or Melodic Statement

Is the melodic idea short or long? What we notice first about Beethoven's Symphony No. 5 is the shortness of the opening statement. The motive . . . —, or "V" in Morse code, has been interpreted as meaning "V" for the Roman numeral five, and "V" for victory, even though Samuel Morse did not invent his code until a decade after Beethoven's death. Wagner, on the other hand, spun seemingly endless melodies in his operas *Tristan and Isolde* and *Parsifal.*

Ornamentation

Melodies are often ornamented with trills and running notes to make them more interesting. Eighteenth-century composers such as Vivaldi, Bach, Handel, Mozart, and Haydn used a great deal of melodic embellishment. Listen to the second movement of Bach's Brandenburg Concerto No. 2.

Imitation

Most concert music contains imitation. Melodies or fragments of melodies are often repeated in another voice or instrument. Try following a melody as it is passed around a chorus or orchestra. The opening of Beethoven's Symphony No. 5 with its . . .— theme is a clear example of imitation. First, the opening theme is stated by the whole orchestra. Then it is passed to different instruments. You will also hear imitation when you listen to Handel's chorus "For Unto Us a Child Is Born" from *Messiah* and to any of Bach's Brandenburg Concertos.

Sequence

Here, the melody or part of it is restated in the *same* instrument or voice using different pitches. Sequences help create unity in the music. We become familiar with the melody in its original form and then recognize it as it recurs with changes of pitch. In the second movement of Beethoven's Symphony No. 7 you can easily follow the sequences.

Type of Scale

Most melodies in Western concert music, particularly music composed before the 20th century, are based on pitches of the major and minor scales. In general, the major scale has a bright, happy quality, while the minor scale has a more plaintive quality.

Early twentieth-century composers developed both new scales and new uses of older scales to give their music freshness. Similar innovations were happening in the other arts. Debussy and Ravel were influenced by the Asian music they heard at the Paris World's Fair. As a result, they began utilizing pentatonic, chromatic, and whole-tone scales.

The *pentatonic* scale is a five-note scale most often used in Asian music. The *chromatic* is constructed entirely of half steps, and the *whole-tone* scale, entirely of whole steps. Listen to Debussy's *Afternoon of a Faun* and you will hear all three scales.

HARMONY

Consonant or Dissonant?

Consonant harmonies are perceived by the listener as restful, balanced, and pleasing. Dissonant harmonies may seem harsh to most listeners.

Chords

A chord is the simultaneous sounding of three or more pitches. Major and minor chords are made up of intervals of thirds (every other note of a scale). Chords with pitches close together (mostly seconds) are called "clusters." You might hear a cluster if a cat jumps on a piano. Chords with gaps of fourths are called "quartal harmony."

Polychords

Some twentieth-century composers superimposed two or more chords—similar to a double exposure on a photograph. Stravinsky used polychords in *The Rite of Spring* and *Petrushka.*

TONALITY

Most music you will hear in the concert hall has a tonal center or home base. This is also referred to as the *key.* The titles give an indication of work's tonality; for example, Beethoven's Symphony No. 5 in c minor, Mozart's Symphony No. 41 in C Major, and Tchaikovsky's Piano Concerto No. 1 in b-flat minor.

Phillippe Entremont, pianist (Courtesy of ICM Artists LTD./Photo by Eleanor Morrison)

Sections in most concert music are in either major or minor tonality. Occasionally the music has contrasting sections that shift back and forth between major and minor. The second movement of Haydn's Symphony No. 94 is a series of playful variations that contains a juxtaposition of major and minor tonalities with the same melody. Many symphonies by Haydn and Mozart present a first theme in major and a second theme in minor, or vice versa, thereby adding contrast and interest to the music.

Atonality

Tone-row, twelve-tone, or serial music is designed to sound "atonal," without a tonal center, like Webern's *Six Pieces for Orchestra*. If you are completely bound to traditional tonal music, you may feel a little lost with this music. Since atonal music uses a somewhat different musical language, you may need time to become familiar with that language.

Polytonality

Similar to polychords, polytonality utilizes two or more tonalities or keys played at the same time. Like the double exposure in photography in which you perceive two different but recognizable subjects, polytonality superimposes tonalities to create an entirely different impression from that created by each tonality on its own. To hear polytonality, listen to Stravinsky's suites from his ballets *Petrushka* and *The Rite of Spring*.

TEXTURE

Composers create a musical fabric out of the materials at their disposal. How they choose to layer their musical ideas creates the texture.

Monophonic

A melody alone without any other melodic line or accompaniment. When you sing in the shower, you are using a monophonic texture.

Homophonic

This is the predominant texture used in both concert music and popular music. Here, the melody is supported by a harmonic accompaniment. A folk singer accompanying himself on guitar is using a homophonic texture. A hymn sung in church with an organ accompaniment is another example.

Polyphonic

Several melodies or melodic lines moving against each other make up the polyphonic texture. A round such as "Row, Row, Row Your Boat," with voices entering at different times and with an overlapping of parts, is an example of polyphony. Sections of music with a great deal of imitation are also using a polyphonic texture. Pachelbel's Canon and all the choruses from Handel's *Messiah* are examples of this texture.

FORM

For an explanation of form, refer to Chapter 3.

TIPS ON IMPROVING YOUR LISTENING

1. *Listen to as much music and as many different styles of music as possible*. The more familiar you are with a piece of music, the more you will discover its subtleties. Once you are familiar with musical styles, you will be able to predict the possible directions a piece of music will take, even if you have not heard it before.

2. *Focus your concentration on the music.* Try to follow the melodies and other musical ideas as they weave through the music. At a concert, do not allow yourself to be distracted by all the people and ambient noise or to get caught up in the actions of the conductor or performers. It is also possible to relax too much and just daydream, take a sound bath, or nod off. There is always something to concentrate on. If you study the "Music Listening Guide," you will be able to put it to work for you.

3. *Gather as much information as you can about the music.* Sources such as magazines, books, record jackets, program notes, and lectures are readily available (see Appendix E). Find out why a particular work was composed, what the composer had in mind, and how various performers think and feel about the piece. Knowing these things helps make you informed.

4. *Delay your judgment of the music till you know it well.* Great art often has many levels of depth. Naturally, it takes time and familiarity for them to unfold. You will cheat yourself if you write off a particular piece of music after just one hearing. Apply all the listening techniques before you make up your mind. You may still conclude that you do not like it and do not want to hear it again, but at least you will have given the music a fair chance. More likely, you will develop an enjoyment and appreciation of that music through subsequent hearings.

CODA

I have given you a map leading to buried treasure—the great masterpieces of music. As you listen now to a piece of music, you will begin to realize how all the musical elements interact to create a work of art. It may take a while for all your discoveries to come together, but there is no rush. The journey and discoveries are the joy. Great concert music will not disappear. It is your legacy. Enjoy your adventure.

BASIC RECORD COLLECTION

This list of great musical works will assist you in constructing your personal record library. There are many excellent recordings, including new releases, from which to choose.

When purchasing recordings, compare different discs and tapes. Since compact discs often contain up to 110 minutes of music, you may find discs that contain several of the recommended works.

Also, consult the Schwann catalog of recordings at your local record store. It lists composers, their compositions and recordings that are available.

WHICH RECORDS SHOULD I PURCHASE FIRST?

The Recommended Basic Record Library is divided into four parts to assist you in purchasing records:

A	Starter Set (approximately 10 compact discs)
B	Expanded Set (approximately 10 additional compact discs)
C	Specialized Set (approximately 10 compact discs)
D	Connoisseur Set—the rest of the recordings to complete your basic record library

RECOMMENDED BASIC RECORD LIBRARY

Bach	**C**	*Brandenburg* Concerto No. 1 in F Major
	A	*Brandenburg* Concerto No. 2 in F Major
	D	*Brandenburg* Concerto No. 3 in G Major
	D	*Brandenburg* Concerto No. 4 in G Major
	A	*Brandenburg* Concerto No. 5 in D Major
	D	*Brandenburg* Concerto No. 6 in B-Flat Major
	B	Cantata No. 140 *(Wachet auf)*

	D	*Christmas Oratorio*
	C	Mass in B Minor
Bartòk	C	*Concerto for Orchestra*
	D	*Music for Strings, Percussion and Celesta*
Beethoven	B	Piano Concerto No. 3 in C Minor
	A	Piano Concerto No. 5 in E-Flat Major *Emperor)*
	B	Violin Concerto in D Major
	D	Piano Sonata No. 8 in C Minor *(Pathétique)*
	D	String Quartet Opus 18 No. 1 in F Major
	D	String Quartet Opus 18 No. 2 in G Major
	D	String Quartet Opus 18 No. 3 in D Major
	D	String Quartet Opus 18 No. 4 in C Minor
	D	String Quartet Opus 18 No. 5 in A Major
	D	String Quartet Opus 18 No. 6 B-Flat Major
	D	String Quartet Opus 59 No. 1 in F Major
	D	String Quartet Opus 59 No. 2 in E Minor
	D	String Quartet Opus 59 No. 3 in C Major
	B	Symphony No. 3 in E-Flat Major *(Eroica)*
	A	Symphony No. 5 in C Minor
	C	Symphony No. 6 in F Major *(Pastoral)*
	B	Symphony No. 7 in A Major
	B	Symphony No. 9 in D Minor *(Choral)*
Berg	D	Violin Concerto
Berlioz	D	*Requiem*
	D	*Roman Carnival Overture*
	A	*Symphonie fantastique*
Bernstein	D	*Candide* Overture
	D	*Fancy Free* (ballet)
	D	*Mass*
	D	*On the Town* (ballet)
	C	*West Side Story*
Bizet	D	*Carmen* (opera and orchestral suite)
	D	Symphony No. 1 in C Major
Brahms	A	*Academic Festival Overture*
	D	*Alto Rhapsody*
	B	Piano Concerto No. 1 in D Minor
	C	Violin Concerto in D Major
	B	Symphony No. 1 in C Minor
	C	Symphony No. 2 in D Major
	D	Symphony No. 3 in F Major

	D	Symphony No. 4 in E Minor
Britten	C	*Young Person's Guide to the Orchestra*
Carlos	D	*By Request* (electronic)
Chopin	D	Piano Concerto No. 1 in E Minor
	A	Piano music (études, mazurkas, preludes, etc.)
Copland	A	*Appalachian Spring*
	C	Suite from *Billy the Kid*
	B	Suite from *Rodeo*
Debussy	B	*Afternoon of a Faun*
	D	*La Mer*
Dvořák	A	Cello Concerto in B Minor
	D	Symphony No. 9 in E Minor *(New World)*
Gershwin	B	*An American in Paris*
	B	Piano Concerto in F Major
	B	*Rhapsody in Blue*
	D	*Porgy and Bess* (complete opera or highlights)
Grieg	C	Piano Concerto in A Minor
Handel	C	*Messiah*
Haydn	D	Symphony No. 88 in G Major
	A	Symphony No. 94 in G Major *(Surprise)*
	C	Symphony No. 101 in D Major *(Clock)*
	D	*The Creation* (oratorio)
Ives	D	*Symphony: Holidays*
	D	*Three Places in New England*
Mahler	D	*Das Lied von der Erde* (song cycle)
	B	*Songs of a Wayfarer*
	A	Symphony No. 1 in D Major *(Titan)*
	D	Symphony No. 4 in G Major
Mendelssohn	A	Violin Concerto in E Minor
	D	*A Midsummer Night's Dream* (incidental music)
Mozart	A	Piano Concerto No. 21 in C Major
	D	*Don Giovanni* (opera)
	D	Symphony No. 35 in D Major *(Haffner)*
	A	Symphony No. 40 in G Minor
	A	Symphony No. 41 in C Major *(Jupiter)*
Mussorgsky	B	*A Night on Bald Mountain*
	C	*Pictures at an Exhibition*
Prokofiev	D	*Lieutenant Kije Suite*

	D	*Peter and the Wolf*
	B	Symphony No. 1 in D Major *(Classical)*
Puccini	C	*La Bohème* (opera)
	D	*Madame Butterfly* (opera)
Rachmaninoff	C	Piano Concerto No. 2 in C Minor
Ravel	B	*Bolero*
	D	Piano Concerto in G Major
Rimsky-Korsakov	D	*Scheherazade*
Schoenberg	D	*Five Pieces for Orchestra*
Schubert	D	Art Songs
	D	Quintet in A Major *(Trout)*
	C	Symphony No. 8 in B Minor *(Unfinished)*
	D	Symphony No. 9 in C Major *(Great)*
Schumann	D	*Carnaval* (piano solo)
	A	Piano Concerto in A Minor
	D	*Dichterliebe* (songs)
	C	Symphony No. 1 in B-Flat Major *(Spring)*
Shostakovich	D	Symphony No. 5
Sibelius	D	Violin Concerto in D Minor
	D	*Finlandia*
	D	Symphony No. 2 in D Major
Smetana	D	*The Moldau*
Strauss, R.	D	*Death and Transfiguration (Tod und Verklärung)*
	B	*Don Juan*
	D	*Ein Heldenleben (A Hero's Life)*
	D	*Till Eulenspiegel's Merry Pranks (Till Eulen spiegels lustige Streiche)*
Stravinsky	D	*Firebird Suite*
	D	*L'Histoire du soldat (Story of a Soldier)*
	B	Petrushka Suite
	A	*The Rite of Spring (Le Sacre du printemps)*
	D	*Symphony of Psalms*
Tchaikovsky	D	*Capriccio Italien*
	A	Piano Concerto No. 1 in B-Flat Minor
	A	Violin Concerto in D Major
	D	*The Nutcracker* Suite
	D	*1812 Overture*
	D	*Swan Lake* (excerpts)
	C	Symphony No. 4 in F Minor
	B	Symphony No. 5 in E Minor

	C	Symphony No. 6 in B Minor *(Pathétique)*
Varèse	D	*Density 21.5*
	D	*Ionisation*
Verdi	D	*Aida* (opera)
	D	*Requiem*
	D	*Rigoletto* (opera)
	D	*La Traviata* (opera)
Vivaldi	D	Concerto in C Major for Two Trumpets
	D	Concerti for Violin
	B	*The Four Seasons*
Wagner	B	Overtures, preludes, and incidental music: *The Flying Dutchman, Lohengrin, Die Meistersinger von Nürnberg, Parsifal, Der Ring des Nibelungen, Tannhäuser, Tristan und Isolde*
Weber	D	*Invitation to the Dance*
	D	Overture to *Euryanthe*
		Overture to *Der Freischütz*
		Overture to *Oberon*
Webern	D	*Five Movements for String Quartet*

CLASSICAL MUSIC RADIO STATIONS AND TEXACO METROPOLITAN OPERA BROADCASTS IN NORTH AMERICA

Explanation   The listings below come from several sources. The opera broadcasts are indicated with the symbol®. Since the directories list radio stations with predominantly classical music formats, stations that mix their formats are not included. For instance, many college and university stations air classical music for only a portion of their broadcast day and, therefore, may not appear in the list. Also, shifting demographics and economics cause many stations to change their formats on short notice. Those stations may not be listed at the time of this book's publication.

STATION	AM	FM
ALABAMA		
Andalusia WKYD	920	
Birmingham WBHM		90.3*
Decatur WRSA		96.9
Dothan WRWA		88.7*
Huntsville WNDA		95.1*
Mobile WHIL		91.3*
Montgomery/ WTSU		89.9*
Opp		
Troy WAMI	860*	
Tuscaloosa WQPR		88.7
ALASKA		
Anchorage KSKA		91.1*
Central K219AD		97.7*
Delta K219AQ		91.7*
Excursion Inlet K210AS		89.9*
Fairbanks KUAC		104.7*
Glenallen K221BL		92.1*
Glenallen KCAM	790	
Gustavus K201AM		88.1*
Healy K269AD		101.7*
Hoonah K220BT		91.1*
Juneau KTOO		104.3*
Lemon Creek K269AO		101.7*
Nenana K216AN		91.1*
Palmer K208BC		89.5*
Seward K201AO		88.1*
Unalaska K216BG		91.1*
Unalaska KIAL	1450	
Valley/Auke Bay K276AF		103.1*
ARIZONA		
Douglas KAPR	930*	
Duncan K208BT		89.5*
Flagstaff KNAU		88.7*
Fountain Hills K276BZ		103.1*
Kingman KNAU		89.7*
Page KNAU		89.7*

STATION	AM	FM
Phoenix KONC		106.3*
Phoenix K208BU		89.5*
Prescott KNAU		90.9*
Sierra Vista KUAT		89.7*
Springville KQAZ		101.7*
Tucson KUAT		90.5*
Tucson K209AF		89.7*
Yuma KAWC		88.9*
ARKANSAS		
Batesville KUAR		94.7*
El Dorado KBSA		90.9*
Fayetteville KUAF		91.3*
Forest City KUAR		94.7*
Fort Smith KWHN	1320*	
Hope KUAR		106.9*
Jonesboro KASU		91.9*
Little Rock KUAR		89.1*
Monticello KUAR		106.9*
Russellville KXRI		91.9*
CALIFORNIA		
Alturas KUNR		97.7*
Arcata KHSU		90.5*
Bakersfield KPMC	1560	
Bakersfield KIWI		92.1
Big Bend KSOR		91.3*
Bishop KUNR		90.9*
Burney K215BJ		90.9*
Callahan K206AN		89.1*
Chester KCHO		91.7*
Chico KCHO		91.1*
Crescent City KSOR		91.7*
Davis K257CU		99.3*
Fresno KBIF	900*	
Ft. Jones/Etna K216BD		91.1*
Gasquet KSOR		91.1*
Happy Camp KSOR		91.9*
Los Angeles KCPB		91.1

STATION	AM	FM
Los Angeles KCRW		89.9
Los Angeles KKGO		105.1
Los Angeles KPSC		88.7
Los Angeles KUSC		91.5*
Marysvill/Yuba Cty K220AG		91.9*
McCloud/Dunsuir KSOR		88.3*
Modesto KHYV	970*	
Monterey KBOQ		92.7
Northridge KCSN		88.5
Pacific Grove KAZU		90.3*
Palm Springs KPSL	1010	
Palm Springs KPSC		88.5*
Philo KZYX		90.7
Quincy KCMT		98.9
Redding KCHO		88.7*
Redding KSOR		90.9*
Red Bluff KCHO		91.5
Ridgecrest KVCR		88.7*
Sacramento KSAC	1240	
Sacramento KXPR		90.9*
San Bernardino KVCR		91.9*
San Diego KFSD		94.1*
San Diego KPBS		89.5
San Francisco KDFC	1220	102.1
San Francisco KKHI	1550	95.7*
San Francisco KUSF		90.3
San Luis Obispo KCPR		91.3*
Santa Barbara KDB	1490	93.7*
Santa Barbara KFAC		88.7*
Santa Maria KGDP	660*	
South Lake Tahoe K201AJ		88.1*
Stockton KUOP		91.3
Thousand Oaks KUPB		91.1*
Weaverville KCHO		89.5*
Weed KSOR		89.5*
Yreka/Montague KSOR		91.5*

	STATION	AM	FM
CANADA			
English Stereo Network			
Altona	CFAM	950	
Altona	CJRB	1220	
Brandon	CBC		92.7*
Cape Breton(Sydney)	CBC		105.1*
Calgary	CBC		102.1*
Cobourg	CFMX		96.3
Cobourg	CFMX		103.1
Edmonton	CBC		90.09*
Edmonton	CKUA	580	
Edmonton	XKU		94.9
Fredericton	CBC		101.5*
Halifax	CBC		102.7*
Kingston	CBC		92.9*
Lethbridge	CBC		91.7*
London	CBC		100.5*
Metchosin	CBC		105.1*
Moncton	CBC		95.5*
Moncton	CBAF		88.5
Middleton	CBC		93.3*
Montreal	CBC		93.5*
Ottawa	CBC		103.3*
Ottawa	CBOF		102.9
Ottawa	CBOF	1250	
Peterborough	CBC		103.9*
Regina	CBC		96.9*
Saskatoon	CBC		105.5*
St. John's	CBC		106.9*
St. John's	VOWR	800	
Thunder Bay	CBC		101.7*
Toronto	CBC		94.1*
Vancouver	CBC		105.7*
Windsor	CBC		89.9*
Winnipeg	CBC		98.3*
French Stereo Network			
Chicoutimi	CBJ		100.9*
Moncton	CBAL		98.3*
Ottawa	CBOX		102.5*
Quebec City	CBV		95.3*
Quebec City	CKRL		89.1
Rimouski	CJBR		101.5*
Trois Rivieres	CBF		104.3*
COLORADO			
Aspen	KVOD		101.7*
Aspen	KSNO	1260	
Boulder	KVOD		101.7*
Carbondale	KVOD		100.9*
Colorado Springs	KCME		88.7*
Colorado Springs	KKCS	1460	
Colorado Springs	DDCS		101.9
Craig	KVOD		106.3*
Denver	KYGO		98.5
Denver	KVOD		99.5*
Durango	KIUP	930*	
Eagle	K210AD		89.9*
Estes Park	KVOD		92.7*
Fort Collins	KVOD		96.7*
Fort Collins	KCSU		90.5
Glenwood Springs	KVOD		105.5*
Glenwood Springs	K205AZ		88.9*
Grand Junction	KPRN		89.5
Greeley	KUNC		91.5
Leadville	KVOD		102.3*
Montrose	KKXK		94.1*
Nucla/Naturita	KKXK		99.3*
Ouray	KURA		104.9
Paronia/Hotchkiss	KKXK		99.3*
Ridgeway	KKXK		99.3*
Steamboat Springs	KVOD		98.3*
Telluride	KKXK		94.3*
Thomasville	KVOD		106.3*
Westminster	KPOE	910	
CONNECTICUT			
Bloomfield	WJMJ		88.9
Fairfield	WSHU		91.1
Hartford	WEDW		88.5
Hartford	WPKT		90.5*
Monroe	WMNR		88.1
Monroe	WRXC		90.1
New Caanan	WSLX		91.9
New London	WNPR		89.1*
Stamford	WQXR		103.1*
Stamford	WFDW		88.5*
DISTRICT OF COLUMBIA			
Washington	WGMS		103.5*
FLORIDA			
Daytona	WSBB	1230*	
Delray Beach	WSBB	1420*	
Fort Myers	WSFP		90.1*
Fort Pierce	WQCS		88.9
Gainesville	WUFT		89.1*
Jacksonville	WJCT		89.9*
Key West	WKRY		93.5*
Miami/Ft. Lauderdale/			
Palm Beach	WTMI		93.1*
Orlando	WTLN	16520*	
Orlando	WUCF		89,9*
Pensacola	WUWF		88.1
Panama City	WKGC		90.7*
Tallahassee	WFSQ		91.5*
Tampa	WBVM		90.5
Tampa/			
St. Petersburg	WUSE		89.7*
GEORGIA			
Albany	WGPC		104.5*
Albany	WUNV		91.7*
Athens	WUGA		91.7*
Atlanta	WABE		90.1*
Atlanta	WGKA	1190	
Atlanta	WREK		91.1
Augusta	WACG		90.7*
Columbus	WRCG	1420*	
Columbus	WTJB		91.7*
Gainesville	WBCX		89.1*
Macon	WNEX	1400*	
Macon/Cochran	WDCO		89.7*
Savannah	WSVH		91.1*
Tifton	WABR		91.1*
Valdusta	WVVS		90.9
Valdusta	WWET		91.7*
Warm Spring	WJSP		88.1*
Waycross	WACL	570*	
Waycross	WXVS		90.1*
HAWAII			
Haleiwa/			
Schofield Bay	K204BB		88.7*
Honolulu	KHPR		88.1*
Wailuku	KKUA		90.7*
IDAHO			
Blackfoot	K216CG		91.1*
Boise	KJHY		102.0*
Boise	KBSU	730*	
Boise	KBSU		90.3
Bonners Ferry	KPBX		91.9*
Burley	K280DV		103.9*
Cote d'Alene	KPBX		91.9*
Hailey/Sun Valley	KSKI	1340*	
Kellogg	KPBX		91.9*
McCall	KBSM		91.7
Pocatello	K285CO		104.9*
Rexburg/Idaho Falls	KRIC		100.5*
Sand point	KPBX		101.7*
Twin Falls	KBSW		91.7
Twin Falls/Jerome	K252CZ		98.3*
ILLINOIS			
Carbondale	WSIU		91.9*
Champaign/Urbana	WILL		90.9*
Chicago	WFMT		98.7*
Chicago	WNIB		97.1
Chicago	WNIZ		96.9
DeKalb	WNIU		89.5*
Elgin	WEPS		88.9
Galesburg	WVKC		90.5*
Macomb	WIUM		91.3*
Normal	WGLT		89.1
Peoria	WCBU		89.9*
Quincy	WWQC		90.3*
Rock Island	WVIK		90.3*
Rockford	WNIU		89.5
Weaton	WFTN		88.1
INDIANA			
Ashley	WSSW		94.3
Bloomington	WFIU		103.7*
Evansville	WNIN		88.3*
Fort Wayne	WBNI		89.1*
Goshen	WGCS		91.1
Indianapolis	WAJC		104.5*
Indianapolis	WFYI		90.1
Indianapolis	WICR		88.7
Indianapolis	WSYW	810	107.1
Lafayette	WBAA	920*	
Manchester	WBKE		89.5*
Muncie	WBST		92.1*
Notre Dame	WSND		88.9
Rensselaer	WRIN	1560*	
Richmond	WECI		91.5*
South Bend	WSND		88.9*
Terre Haute	WISU		89.7*
West Lafayette	WBAA	920	
IOWA			
Ames	WOI		90.1*
Cedar Falls	KHKE		89.5
Cedar Falls	KUNI		90.9
Council Bluffs	KIWR		89.7
Decorah	KLCD		90.1*
Decorah	KWLC	1240	
Des Moines	KWKY	1150*	
Fort Dodge	KTPR		91.1
Iowa City	KSUI		91.7*
Sioux City	KWIT		90.3*
KANSAS			
Atchison	K209BB		89.7*
Coffeyville	KGGF	690*	
Colby	KXXX	790*	
Emporia	KANU		90.5*
Hutchinson	KHCC		90.1*
Hutchinson	KHCD		89.5
Iola/Humboldt	KANU		88.1*
Kansas City	KXTR		96.5
Larned	KANS	1510*	
Lawrence	KANU		91.5*
Liberal	KYUU	1470*	
Manhattan	KANU		90.5*
Salinas	KHCD		89.5*
Ulysses	KULY	1420*	
Ulysses	KEXX		106.7*
KENTUCKY			
Bowling Green	WKYU		88.9*
Elizabethtown	WKUE		90.9*
Georgetown	WRVG		89.9
Hazard	WEKH		90.9
Henderson	WKPB		89.5*
Lexington	WUKY		89.5*
Louisville	WFPK		91.9*
Louisville	WUOL		90.5
Murray	WKMS		91.3
Owensboro	WKWC		90.3
Richmond	WEKU		88.9
Somerset	WDCL		89.7*
Vancleve	WMTC	730	99.9
LOUSIANA			
Alexandria	KLSA		90.7*
Baton Rouge/			
Greenwell Springs	WRFK		89.3*
Hammond	KSLU		90.9*
Lafayette	KRVS		88.7*
Lake Charles	K213A		90.5*
Monroe	KEDM		90.3*
Morgan City	KMRC	1430*	
New Orleans	WWNO		89.9*
Shreveport	KDAQ		89.9*
MAINE			
Bangor	WMEH		90.9*
Calais	WMED		89.7*
Millinocket	WSYY	1240*	
Portland	WMEA		90.1*
Presque Isle	WMEM		106.1*
Scarborough	WPKM		106.3*
Waterville/Augusta	WMEW		91.3*
Waterville	WMHB		90.5
MARYLAND			
Baltimore	WBJC		91.5*
Baltimore	WJHU		88.1
Cumberland	WCBC	1270*	
Frostburg	WFWM		91.7
Rockville	WGTS		91.9
Salisbury	WSCL		89.5*
Takoma Park	WGTS		91.9
MASSACHUSETTS			
Amherst	WFCR		88.5
Beverly	WBOQ		104.9
Boston	WCRB		102.5*
Hyannis	WQRC		99.9
Northfield	WNMH		91.5
Pittsfield	WBRK	1340*	
Tisbury	WMVY		92.7
Waltham	WCRB		102.5*
West Chatham	WFCC		107.5*
Worcester	WICN		90.5
MICHIGAN			
Alpena	WCML		91.7*
Ann Arbor	WUOM		91.7
Berrien Springs	WAUS		90.7
Detroit	WQRS		105.1*
East Jordan	WIZY		100.9*
East Lansing	WKAR		90.5*
Escanaba	W218AG		91.5*
Flint	WFBE		95.1*
Flint	WFUM		91.1
Grand Rapids	WVGR		104.1
Houghton	WGGL		91.1*
Interlocken	WIAA		88.7*
Kalamazoo	WMUK		102.1*
Manistique	W220AJ		91.9*
Marquette	MNMU		90.1*
Mount Pleasant	WCMU		89.5*

	STATION	AM	FM
Newberry	W2616AI		91.1*
Saulte Ste/Marie	WCMZ		98.3*
Southfield	WQRS		105.1
Twin Lake	WBLV		90.3*
MINNESOTA			
Austin	K232AQ		94.3*
Bemidji	KCRB		88.5
Buhl	WIRR		90.9*
Brainerd	KBPR		90.7*
Duluth	WIRR		90.9
Duluth/Superior	WSCD		92.9*
Ely	W269AC		101.7*
Fargo/Moorhead	KCCM		91.1*
International Falls	K249BK		97.7*
Minneapolis/St. Paul	KSJN		99.5*
Minneapolis/St. Paul	KUOM	770	
Moorhead	KCCM		91.1
Morris	K257AH		99.3*
Northfield	WCAL		89.3
Rochester/Decorah	KLSE		91.7*
St. Cloud	KSJR		90.1*
St. Peter/Mankato	KFAC		90.5*
Thief River Falls	KQMN		91.5*
Winona	KRSW		91.7*
Worthington/			
Marshall	KRSW		91.7*
MISSISSIPPI			
Aberdeen	WWZQ		105.5*
Ackerman	WMAH		89.9*
Biloxi/McHenry	WMAH		90.3*
Booneville	WMAE		89.5*
Bude	WMAU		88.9*
Greenwood/Inverness	WMAO		90.9*
Hattiesburg	WUSM		88.5*
Holly Springs	WURC		88.1
Jackson	WJTR		90.1
Jackson	WMPN		91.3*
Kosciusko	WKOZ	1340*	
Meridian	WMAW		88.1*
Oxford	WMAV		90.3*
Senatobia	WKNA		88.9*
Starkville	WSSO	1230*	
MISSOURI			
Brookfield	KZBK		96.9*
Columbia	KBIA		91.3*
El Dorado Springs	KESM		105.5*
Joplin	KXMS		88.7*
Joplin	K202AN		88.3*
Kansas City	KCUR		89.3
Kansas City	KXTR		96.5*
Kirkville	K210AU		89.0*
Maryville	KXCV		90.5*
Point Lookout	KCOZ		90.5*
Rolla	KUMR		88.5*
St. Louis	KFUO		99.1*
Springfield	KSMU		91.1
Warrensburg	KCMW		90.9*
MONTANA			
Big Sky	KEMC		95.9*
Big Timber	KEMC		90.5*
Billings	KEMC		91.7*
Bozeman	KBMC		102.1*
Butte	KXTL	1370*	
Butte	KUFM		99.3*
Chester	KEMC		100.1*
Colstrip	KEMC		88.5*
Columbus	KEMC		88.5*
Dillon	K288DZ		105.5*
Glendive	KEMC		88.5*
Great Falls	KGPR		89.9*
Hardin	KEMC		88.5*
Havre	KPQX		92.5*
Havre	KEMC		90.1*
Helena	KUFM		91.7*
Kalispell	KALS		97.1
Lewistown	KEMC		88.5*
Livingston	KEMC		88.5*
Marysville	KUFM		107.1*
Miles City	KEMC		90.7*
Missoula	KUFM		89.1*
Paradise Valley	KEMC		91.1*
Red Lodge	KEMC		89.1*
Swan Lake	KUFM		91.1*
Terry	KEMC		91.9*
White Sulpher Spring	KUFM		98.3*
White Fish	KUFM		91.7*
Wolf Mountain	KEMC		88.5*
NEBRASKA			
Alliance	KTNE		91.1*
Bassett	KMNE		90.3*
Chadron	KCNE		91.9*
Fairbury	KGMT	1310*	
Hastings	KHNE		89.1*

	STATION	AM	FM
Lexington	KLNE		88.7*
Lincoln	KUCV		90.9*
Merriman	KRNE		91.5*
Norfolk	KXNE		89.3*
North Platte	KPNE		91.7*
Omaha	KIOS		91.5*
Omaha	KVNO		90.7*
NEVADA			
Beatty	KNPR		91.7*
Boulder City	KNPR		88.7*
Hawthorne	KUNR		91.5*
Incline Village	KUNR		89.9*
Indian Springs	K204AP		88.7*
Las Vegas	KNPR		89.5*
Laughlin	KNPR		89.5*
Lovelock	KUNR		89.9*
Mesquite	KNPR		89.0*
Moapa Valley	KNPR		88.7*
Pahrump	KNPR		88.7*
Panaca	KLNR		91.7*
Reno	KUNR		88.7*
Scotty's Junction	KNPR		88.1*
Searchlight	KNPR		88.5*
Tonopah	KTPH		91.7*
Verdi	KUNR		91.7*
Winnemucca	KUNR		91.3*
Yerington/			
Smith Valley	KUNR		91.9*
NEW HAMPSHIRE			
Concord	WEVO		89.1
NEW JERSEY			
Egg Harbor	WRDR		105.0*
Ocean City	WSLT		106.3
Trenton	WWFM		96.3
Wildwood	WCMC	1230*	
NEW MEXICO			
Albuquerque	KHFM		96.3*
Majamar	KMTH		98.7*
Portales	KENW		89.5*
Roswell	KMHT		91.1*
Ruidoso	KMTH		91.3*
Santa Fe	K244CX		96.7*
Tucumcari	KENW		91.3*
NEW YORK			
Albany	WAMC		90.3*
Albany	WHRL		103.1*
Alexandria Bay	WLSU		88.7*
Binghamton	WSKG		89.3*
Binghamton	WSQG		90.9
Blue Mountain Lake	WSLU		91.7*
Buffalo	WNED		94.5*
Canajoharie	WCAN		93.3*
Canton	WSLU		89.5*
Corning	WSKG		90.7*
East Syracuse	WVOA		105.1
Ellmira	WSKG		91.1*
Fort Drum	WSLU		88.5*
Ithaca	WSQG		90.9*
Jamestown	WNJA		89.7*
Kingston	WAMK		90.9*
Lake Placid	WSLU		91.7*
Middletown	WOSR		91.7*
New York	WKCR		89.9*
New York	WNCN		104.3
New York	WNYC		93.9
New York	WQXR	1560	96.3*
Nyack	WNYK		88.7
Olean	WHDL	1450*	
Oneanta/Cooperstown	WSQC		91.7*
Rochester	WRUR		88.5
Rochester	WXXI		91.5*
Saranac Lake	WSLU		91.7*
Southampton	WPBX		91.3*
Syracuse	WCNY		91.3*
Ticonderoga	WANC		103.9*
Utica	WUNY		89.5*
Vestal	WSKG		89.7*
Watertown	WJNY		90.9*
Watertown	WSLU		88.5*
Watkins Glen	WSKG		91.1*
NORTH CAROLINA			
Ashville	WCQS		88.1
Ashville	WFQS		91.3
Belmont/Charlotte	WCGC	1270*	
Chapel Hill	WUNC		91.5
Charlotte	WRFX		99.7
Dallas	WSGE		91.7
Davidson/Charlotte	WDAV		89.9*
Fayetteville	WFSS		89.1
Kingston	WKNS		90.5
New Bern	WTEB		89.3*
Wake Forest/Raleigh	WCPE		89.7*

	STATION	AM	FM
Washington	WRRF	930*	
Wilmington	WHQR		91.3*
Winston Salem	WEDD		88.5*
NORTH DAKOTA			
Bismarck	KCND		90.5*
Bismarck	KDPR		89.9
Crary	KFJM		89.5*
Devils Lake	KFJM		91.5*
Dickinson	KDPR		89.9*
Grand Forks	KFJM		89.3*
Lakota	K219AX		91.7*
Minot	KMPR		88.9*
Thief River Falls	KQMW		88.3*
Williston	KPPR		89.5*
OHIO			
Alliance	KRMU		91.1
Athens	WOUB		91.3*
Athens	WOUC		89.1
Athens	WOUL		89.1
Cambridge	WOUC		89.1*
Cincinnati	WCIN	1480	
Cincinnati	WGUG		90.9*
Cleveland	WCLV		95.5*
Columbus	WOSU		89.7*
Dayton	WDPR		89.5*
Ironton	WOUL		89.1*
Kent	WKSU		89.7
Lima	WGLE		90.7*
Mansfield	WOSV		91.7*
Marietta	WMRT		88.3*
Oberlin	WOBC		91.5*
Toledo	WGLE		90.7
Toledo	WGTE		91.3*
Wooster	WCWS		90.9*
Wooster	W224AC		92.7*
Youngstown	WYSU		88.5*
OKLAHOMA			
Oklahoma City	KCSC		90.1*
Stillwater	KOSU		91.7*
Tulsa	KCMA		92.7*
Woodward	KMZE		92.1*
OREGON			
Ashland	KSMF		89.1
Ashland	KSOR		90.1*
Brandon	KSOR		91.7*
Bend	KWAX		88.1*
Brookings	KSOR		91.1*
Camas Valley	KSOR		88.7*
Canyonville	KSOR		91.9*
Chiloquin	KSOR		91.7*
Coos Bay	KSOR		89.1*
Coos Bay/N. Bend	K228CW		93.5*
Coquille	KSOR		88.1*
Corvallis	KOAC	550	
Dead Indian	KSOR		88.1*
Enterprise	K208AE		89.5*
Eugene	KSKF		90.1
Eugene	KWAX		91.1*
Florence	K202BA		88.3*
Fort Jones, Etna	KSOR		91.1*
Gold Beach	KSOR		91.5*
Granta Pass	KSOR		88.9*
Heppner	KSOR		100.1*
Klamath Falls	KSOR		90.5*
LaPine/Beaver Marsh	KSOR		89.1*
Lake View	KSOR		89.5*
Langlois/Sixes	KSOR		91.3*
Lincoln/Pinehurst	KOSR		88.7*
Medford/			
Jacksonville	KSOR		91.9*
Merrill/Malin	KSOR		91.9*
Milton/Freewater	KSOR		100.1*
Newport	K22VEE		91.9*
Pendleton	KRBM		90.9
Port Oxford	KSOR		90.5*
Portland	KBPS	1450	89.9*
Portland	KBVM		88.3
Portland	KOPB		91.5
Powers	KSOR		91.9*
Roseburg	KSRS		91.5*
Sunriver	K213BH		90.5*
Sutherlin/Glide	KSOR		89.3*
PENNSYLVANIA			
Allentown	WVIA		99.3*
Bethlehem	WLVR		91.3
Erie	WQLN		91.3*
Erie	W285AI		104.9*
Grantham	WVMM		90.7
Grove City	WSAJ	1340	
Harrisburg	WITF		89.5*
Hollidaysburg	WKMC	1370*	
Indiana	WIUP		90.1*

	STATION	AM	FM
Lewisburg	WVIA		100.1*
Philadelphia	WFLN		95.7*
Philadelphia	WHYY		90.9
Pittsburgh	WPIT		101.5*
Pittsburgh	WQED		89.3
Pittsburgh	WWCS	540	
Scranton/			
Wilkes Barre	WVIA		89.9*
Slippery Rock	WSRU		90.1
State College	WPSU		91.1*
Stroudsburg	WVIA		94.3*
Williamsport	WRLC		91.7
Williamsport	WVIA		89.3*
PUERTO RICO			
Mayaguez	WTPM		92.9*
San Juan	WIPR	940*	91.3*
San Juan	WRTU		89.7
RHODE ISLAND			
Kingston	WRIU		90.3
Providence	WDOM		91.3
Providence	WLKW	790*	
Providence	WWAZ	790	
SOUTH CAROLINA			
Aiken	WLJK		89.1*
Beaufort	WJWJ		89.9*
Charleston	WOKE	1340*	
Charleston	WSCI		89.3*
Columbia	WHMC		90.1
Columbia	WLTR		91.3*
Columbia	WRJA		88.1
Conway	WHMC		90.1*
Greenville	WEPR		90.1*
Greenville	WMUU		94.5
Rock Hill	WRHI	1340*	
Rock Hill	WNJC		88.9*
Sumter	WRJA		88.1*
SOUTH DAKOTA			
Aberdeen/Pierpont	KDSD		90.9*
Belle Fourche	K201AP		88.1*
Bison	KRCS		97.7*
Brookings	KESD		88.3*
Edgemont	K216AP		91.1*
Hill City	KRCS		103.9*
Hot Springs	K201AQ		88.1*
Lead	K220BA		91.9*
Lemon	KRCS		97.7*
Lowry	KQSU		91.9*
Pierre/Reliance	KTSD		91.1*
Philip	KRCS		97.7*
Pringle	K220AZ		91.9*
Rapid City	KBHE		89.3*
Sioux Falls	KCSD		90.9*
Sioux Falls	KRSD		88.1*
Spearfish	KRCS		98.0*
Sturgis Rapid City	KRCS		93.1*
Vermillion	KUSD	690*	89.7*
TENNESSEE			
Chattanooga	WUTC		88.1*
Collegedale	WSMC		90.5
Dyersburg	WKNQ		90.7*
Harrogate	WLMU		91.3
Henderson	WFHC		91.5
Jackson	WKND		88.1*
Johnson City	WETS		89.5*
Kingsport	WCSK		90.3

	STATION	AM	FM
Knoxville	WUOT		91.9*
Memphis	WKNO		91.1*
Nashville	WPLN		90.3*
TEXAS			
Abilene	KACU		89.7
Amarillo	KACV		89.9
Andrews	KMTH		90.9*
Austin	KMFA		89.5
Austin	KUT		90.5*
Beaumont	KVLU		91.3*
Brownsville/McAllen	KHID		88.1*
Canyon/Amarillo	KAKS	1550*	
College Station	KAMU		90.9
Commerce	KETR		88.9*
Corpus Christi	KEDT		90.3*
Dallas/Fort Worth	WRR		101.1*
Eastland	WEAS	1590*	97.7*
Edinburg	KRIO	910	
El Paso	KTEP		88.5*
Harlingen	KMBH		88.9*
Houston	KUHF		88.7*
Houston	KRTS		?
Huntsville	KSHU		90.5
Keese	KJCR		88.3
Kilgore	KTPB		88.7*
Killeen	KNCT		91.3
Lubbock	KOHM		89.1*
Lufkin	KLDN		88.9*
Midland	KCRS	550*	
Odessa	KOCV		91.3*
Odessa	KRIL	1410	
Quanah	KIXC	1150*	100.9*
San Antonio	KPAC		88.3*
Seabrook	KRTS		92.1
Waco	KWBU		107.1*
UTAH			
Brigham City	KUSU		88.5*
Cedar City	KGSU		91.1*
Delta/Millard County	KUSU		89.5*
Laketown/			
Garden City	KUSU		89.3*
Logan	KUSU		91.5*
Logan/Cache Valley	KUSU		89.5*
Milford	KUSU		90.7*
Monroe/Wayne	KUSU		91.5*
Park City	KPCW		88.1
Park City	KPCW		91.9
Provo/Salt Lake City	KBYU		89.1*
Randolph/Woodruff	KUSU		91.1*
St. George	KUSU		89.1*
Salt Lake City	KEUR		90.1
Tabiona/Roosevelt	KUSU		106.3*
Vernal/Uintah Cnty	KUSU		89.7*
VERMONT			
Brattleboro	WKVT	1490*	
Burlington	WVPS		107.9*
Colchester	WRVT		88.7
Colchester	WVPS		107.9
Rutland	WRUT		88.7*
White River Junction	WKXE		95.3
Windsor	WVPR		89.5*
VIRGINIA			
Arlington	WETA		90.9
Charlottesville	WVTU		89.3*
Harrisonburg	WEMC		91.7

	STATION	AM	FM
Harrisonburg	WMRA		90.7
Lexington	WLUR		91.5*
Norfolk	WHRO		90.3*
Petersburg	WVST		91.3
Richmond	WCVE		88.9*
Roanoke	WVTE		89.3*
WASHINGTON			
College Place	KGTS		91.3
Omak	KPBX		88.9*
Pullman	KFAE		89.1
Pullman	KRFA		91.7
Pullman	KWSU	1270	
Seattle	KING		89.1*
Seattle	KSER		90.7
Spokane	KPBX		91.1*
Spokane	KPBX		90.7*
Twisp	KPBX		91.9*
WEST VIRGINIA			
Beckley	WVPB		91.7*
Buckhannon	WVPW		88.9
Charleston	WVPN		88.5*
Huntington	WVWV		89.9*
Martinsburg	WVEP		88.9*
Morgantown	WVPM		90.9*
Parkersburg	WVPG		90.3*
Wheeling	WVNP		89.9*
WISCONSIN			
Brule/Superior	WHSA		89.9*
Eau Claire	WUEC		89.7*
Glendale	WFMR		104.9*
Green Bay	WPNE		89.3*
La Crosse	K269BK		101.7*
Madison	WERN		88.7*
Madison	WORT		88.9*
Marinette	W217AA		91/3*
Menomonee	WFMR		98.3
Menomonee	WVSS		90.7*
Milwaukee	WFMR		98.3*
Wausau	WHRM		90.9*
WYOMING			
Afton/Star Valley	K285DF		104.9*
Big Horn Basin	KEMC		91.1*
Buffalo	KEMC		91.9*
Buffalo	KEMC	1450*	
Casper	K204AD		88.7*
Casper	KVOD		90.5*
Cheyenne	K204AD		91.9*
Cody	KEMC		88.5*
Gilette	KEMC		88.7*
Jackson Hole/Wilson	K285CY		104.9*
Jeffrey City	K205BI		88.9*
Lander	K203AU		88.5*
Laramie	KUWR		91.9*
Laramie	KVOD		107.1*
Rawlings	K206AJ		89.1*
Riverton	K215AY		90.9*
Sheridan	KEMC		89.9*
Sinclair	K206AJ		89.1*
Sundance	KRCS		103.7*
Terry	KEMC		91.9*
Thermopolis	KEMC		88.9*
Torrington	K210AF		89.9*
Worland	KEMC		88.5*
Yellowstone Park	KEMC		104.9*

WRITING REPORTS

THE SHORT CONCERT REPORT

1. Attach the program and ticket stub of the performance to your report.
2. Write a one paragraph description of each work. Give your personal reaction to each piece. Descibe the music as well as you can both in your own words and the terms presented in this course.
3. Try to include:

- performing medium (also special instruments and soloists)

- general form (symphony, concerto, dance forms, etc.)

- outstanding features of melody, rhythms, texture, style, etc.

Other Directions:

Do not copy from printed concert programs, music reviews, or record jackets. That is a breach of copyright. Take a pad and pen so you can jot down a few comments after movements or works. This will help you remember the music. If permitted, record the performance with a small, battery-operated tape recorder. That way you can write your notes later and just enjoy the performance.

Note: Some professional concerts prohibit taping.

THE LONG CONCERT REPORT

I. General Directions

A. Ask your instructor to recommend concerts.
B. Select one that interests you.
C. Type your report double space. Make sure your computer printout is legible.
D. Include a bibliography and possibly footnotes.
E. attach your program and ticket stub.

II. Pre-concert Report

Select one major work or a group of short works scheduled on the concert.

A. Present your research on the historical background of:
   1. the composer
   2. the composition
B. Listen to a recording and give your general reaction to the performance and specific reaction to the music regarding the composer's use of:
   1. performing media
   2. rhythmn, tempo, meter
   3. melodic materials
   4. harmony and tonality
   5. textures
   6. form

III. Post-concert review

A. Include background information: date, time, place, performer(s), and musical selections.
B. Discuss your reactions to each work performed. Include both your intellectual and emotional reactions.
C. Discuss your reaction to the quality of the performance and performer(s). Also comment on the concert ritual the performers follow.
D. Compare the live concert performance of the major work with the recorded performance you researched.

Other Directions:

Refrain from giving merely a play-by-play account of the concert; your printed program already gives that information.

Do not copy directly from sources. You may paraphrase researched sources as long as you cite these sources with footnotes and in a bibliography.

Jot notes after movements or works to help you remember the performance. Try not to write during the live performance so that you will not distract yourself and tape recorder to help you write your post-concert review.

THE RESEARCH REPORT

Directions

1. Choose one topic.
   • From the following list of suggested topics, choose one for a research report. Or, choose an alternate topic similar to those suggested. Compare and contrast the musical selections using terminology you learned, research sources, and your experiences attending concerts.

2. Include biographical data on composers.
   • Explain how events in the composer's life relate to the works have chosen to compare.

3. What was happening at the time in society, politics, and economics that influenced the general musical style?
   • Cite specific examples from the music you selected.

4. Include information about the performer and recording.
   • Identify the ensemble, conductor, soloists, and any other performers mentioned on the recording.

   • Identify, if possible, the date of the recording and its production label.

5. Include a bibliography.
   • Cite all sources used to research your topic—books, articles, records.

6. Be original!
   • Do not copy directly from sources: printed concert programs, music reviews, or record jackets. That is a breach of copyright. You may paraphrase resource material as long as you properly cite sources with footnotes and in the bibliography.

Other Directions:

Take a pad and pen so you can jot down a few comments after movements or works. This will help you remember the music. If permitted, record the performance with a small, battery-operated tape recorder. That way you can write your notes later and just enjoy the performance.

Note: Some professional concerts prohibit taping.

SUGGESTED RESEARCH TOPICS

1. Compare and contrast an early and a late work by the same composer:

    • Haydn's Symphony No. 45 (*Farewell,* 1772) and Symphony No. 94 (*Surprise,* 1791)

    • Beethoven's Symphony No.1 (1800) and Symphony No. 9 (*Choral,* 1824)

    • Beethoven's String Quartets Opus 18 and String Quartets Opus 135.

    • Verdi's *Rigoletto* (1851) and *Othello* (1887)

    • Puccini's *La Bohème* (1896) and *Turandot* (posthumous, 1926)

    • Mahler's Symphony No. 1 (*The Titan,* 1888) and Symphony No. 8 (*Symphony of a Thousand,* 1909)

    • Stravinsky's ballet *The Rite of Spring* (1913) and *Ebony Concerto* (1945)

2. Compare and contrast two similar works by two different composers of the same style period:

    • Bach's *Christmas* Oratorio and Handel's *Messiah* Oratorio

    • Brahms's *Academic Festival Overture* and Wagner's *Die Meistersinger von Nürnberg Overture*

    • Tchaikovsky's *Nutcracker* Ballet and Falla's Suite from *The Three Cornered Hat* Ballet

    • Gershwin's *An American in Paris* and Copland's *Appalachian Spring.*

    • Rimsky-Korsakov's *Capriccio espagnole* and Tchaikovsky's *Capriccio italien*

3. Compare and contrast two similar works by two different composers from two different style periods:

    • Haydn's Syphony No. 94 *(Surprise)* and Prokofiev's Symphony No. 1 *(Classical)*

    • Vivaldi's Concerto *(Spring)* from *The Four Seasons* and Schuman's Symphony No. 1 *(Spring)*

- Vivaldi's *The Four Seasons* and Beethoven's Symphony No. 6 *(Pastoral)*

- Bach's *Mass in b minor* and Bernstein's *Mass*

- Beethoven's Symphony No. 9 *(Choral)* and Stravinsky's *The Rite of Spring*

4. Other miscellaneous topics:

  - Discuss the differences in orchestral music in the Classical, Romantic, and 20th-century style periods.

  - Compare the musical contributions of Felix Mendelssohn and Leonard Bernstein.

  - Trace and discuss the development of the concert tradition from the Baroque period to the present.

  - Describe and discuss the various ways that composers and musicians supported themselves from the Baroque period to the present.

  - Describe, compare, and contrast the different ways of listening to music of the Baroque, Classical, and Romantic style periods.

FURTHER READING

Reference

Baker's *Biographical Dictionary of Musicians,* Nicolas Slonimsky, ed. (New York: Schirmer, 1985).

Bookspan, Martin, *101 Masterpieces of Music and Their Composers.* (Garden City, N.Y.: Dophin Books, 1973).

Ferguson, Donald N., *Masterpieces of the Orchestral Repertoire.* (Minneapolis, Minn.: The University of Minnesota Press, 1968).

Harvard Dictionary of Music, ed. Don Randel (Cambridge, Mass.: Harvard UP, 1986)

The New Grove Dictionary of Music and Musicians, ed. Stanley Sadie (Washington, DC: Macmillan, 1980).

Instruments

Anthony Baines, *Musical Instruments through the Ages* (Baltimore: Penguin, 1966).

Robert Donington, *Music and Its Instruments* (New York: Methuen, 1982).

Mary Remnant, *Musical Instruments of the West* (New York: St. Martin's, 1978).

History

Gerald Abraham, *The Concise Oxford History of Music* (New York: Oxford UP, 1980).

Donald Jay Grout, *A History of Western Music* (New York: Norton, 1980).

Style Periods

Claude V. Palisca, *Baroque Music* (Englewood Cliffs, N.J.: Prentice-Hall, 1981).

Charles Rosen, *The Classical Style: Haydn, Mozart, Beethoven* (New York: Norton, 1972).

Leon Plantinga, *Romantic Music* (New York: Norton, 1985)

Bryan Simms, *Music of the Twentieth Century* (New York: Schirmer, 1986).

Paul Griffiths, *A Guide to Electronic Music* (New York: Thames & Hudson, 1979).

Opera

Donald Jay Grout, *A Short History of Opera* (New York: Columbia University Press, 1965).

J. Merrill Knapp, *The Magic of Opera* (New York: Harper and Row, 1972).

General

Aaron Copland, *What to Listen for in Music* (New York: McGraw-Hill, 1957).

Leonard Bernstein, *The Joy of Music* (New York: Simon & Schuster, 1954).

Karl Haas, *Inside Music* (New York: Anchor Books, 1984).

Stanley Sadie, Music guide: An Introduction (Englewood Cliffs, N.J.: Prentice-Hall, 1986).

Jay Zorn, *Listening to Music* (Englewood Cliffs, N.J.: Prentice Hall, 1991).

American Music

James Lincoln Collier, *The Making of Jazz* (New York: Houghton Mifflin, 1978).

Charles Hamm, *Music in the New World* (New York: Norton, 1983).

Hodier, André, *Jazz: Its Evolution and Essence* (New York: Grove, 1956).

Paul Oliver, Max Harrison, and William D. Bolcom, *Ragtime, Blues, and Jazz* [The New Grove](New York: Norton, 1986).

Gunther Schuller, *Early Jazz: Its Roots and Musical Development* (New York: Oxford University Press, 1968).

H. Wiley Hitchcock, *Music in the United States: a Historical Introduction* (Englewood Cliffs, N.J.: Prentice Hall, 1974).

Periodicals

American Record Guide
CD Review
Chamber Music (Chamber Music America)
Dance Magazine
Fanfare
High Fidelity

Musical America
Opera Canada
Opera Guide
Opera News
Opera Quarterly
Opus
Ovation
Stereo Review

Record Listings

Schwann Record and Tape Guide
Schwann Compact Disc Catalog

GLOSSARY
OF MUSICAL TERMS

Absolute music   Music without extramusical associations, program, or literary reference.

A cappella   Choral music without accompaniment.

Accelerando   Gradual quickening of tempo.

Accent   Emphasis on a particular note.

Adagio   Slow tempo.

Air   A tune for voice or instrument.

Allegretto   Less quick than allegro; moderately fast tempo.

Allegro   Fast tempo.

Allemande   A Baroque dance in moderate tempo and two-beat meter.

Alto   A low female voice, also called contralto.

Andante   Moderate, walking tempo.

Andantino   Slightly faster tempo that andante.

Antiphony   Music in which two or more groups are separated to create an echo effect and contrast.

Arco   A string instrument bowing direction where the bow is used as opposed to plucking the string.

Aria   An elaborate solo song with instrumental accompaniment, generally in an opera, oratorio, or cantata.

Arpeggio   Chord tones sounded in succession rather than simultaneously.

Art song   An elaborate solo song, usually composed to an existing poem, sung with accompaniment.

Atonality   Music without tonality or key.

Avante-garde   A French term used to describe radical or advanced composers and other artists.

Ballad   A narrative-style folk song.

Bar   See *measure*.

Baritone   A male voice with a range between tenor and bass.

Bass   The lowest, heaviest male voice.

Basso Continuo   A bass line that provides a basis for a harmonic accompaniment; most often used in Baroque music.

Beat   The underlying basic rhythmic pulse.

Bel canto   A style of singing, particularly in Italian opera, that displays the singer's vocal agility and beautiful tone.

Bolero   A Spanish dance in moderate tempo, three beats per measure.

Bourrée   A fast Baroque dance with two beats per measure.

Bridge   (1) A musical passage between two major sections. (2) The part of a stringed instrument that supports the strings.

Cadence   A melodic or harmonic progression that gives the effect of closing a section.

Cadenza   A virtuoso passage (sometimes imporovised) played by the soloist in a concerto, usually without orchestral accompaniment.

Canon   Music in which one or more lines continue to imitate one another throughout the work.

Cantata   Vocal music developed in the Baroque period for solo voices(s), instruments, and often a chorus; based on a religious or a secular text.

Canzona   A short instrumental piece popular in the sixteenth and seventeenth centuries.

Chaconne   A work featuring variations on a progression of chords repeated throughout the work.

Chamber music   Instrumental music performed by a small ensemble.

Chorale   A hymn tune used in the German Lutheran Church.

Chord   The simultaneous sounding of three or more pitches.

Choreographer   The person who plans the dancer's movements.

Chorus   (1) A group that sings choral music. (2) A section of an opera or oratorio sung by a chorus. (3) The refrain or main section of a song.

Chromatic   A scale or harmonic movement of half steps.

Clavier   A general term indicating any keyboard instrument.

Coda   The Italian word for "tail"; the section that brings the movement to a conclusion.

Coloratura   A virtuoso style of singing, usually including fast scales, arpeggios, ornaments; often associated with a light, high, soprano voice, particularly in opera.

Common time   A meter that consists of four beats per measure.

Concertmaster   (*Konzertmeister* in German) The first chair player in the first violin section of an orchestra.

Concerto   A work for solo instrument(s), usually with three movements, accompanied by an orchestra.

Concerto grosso   A concerto for a small instrumental group accompanied by a small orchestra.

Concert overture   An overture not associated with an opera or drama.

Consonance   A group of sounds that seems pleasing or restful.

Continuo   See *basso continuo*.

Contrabassoon   A large bassoon pitched an octave below the usual bassoon.

Contralto   See *alto*.

Counterpoint   Two or more independent melodic lines occurring at the same time.

Counter subject   The secondary theme in a fugue.

Courante   A lively dance in triple meter and fast tempo.

Crescendo   Gradual increase in volume.

Decrescendo   Gradual decrease in volume. Also called diminuendo.

Development   (1) The process of developing themes. (2) The section in sonata form featuring the development of themes.

Dissonance   A group of sounds that seems disagreeable or unpleasant.

Double stop   The sounding of two different pitches simultaneously on a stringed instrument.

Downbeat   The accented first beat of a measure.

Dynamics   The various levels of intensity or loudness in music.

Electronic music   Music in which sounds are created with or modified by an electronic synthesizer.

Étude   A short instrumental composition concentrating on a particular technical aspect of performance.

Exposition   The opening section of fugue and sonata forms.

Fantasia   A short composition in free form.

Finale   The concluding movement of some multimovement works and operas.

Flat   A sign indicating that a pitch is to be lowered by a half step.

Form   The structure or plan of a composition.

Fugue   A composition in which the main theme is presented in imitation in several parts.

Gavotte   A dance with a moderate tempo in two-beat meter.

Gigue   A Baroque dance in compound meter with a fast tempo.

Glissando   A performance effect provided by rapid sliding up or down scales

Grave   Very slowly and solemnly.

Harmony   The simultaneous sounding of pitches.

Harmonics   (1) Secondary tones that form a part of most tones. (2) High-pitched tones that are produced on a string instrument by placing the finger lightly on a string.

Harpsichord   A popular keyboard instrument of the sixteenth through eighteenth centuries of which the strings are plucked when the keys are depressed.

Homophony   A texture consisting of a line of melody and accompaniment.

Imitation   The repetition of a melody or portion of a melody in another part.

Impromptu   A short piano compositon that sounds improvised.

Improvisation   Spontaneous performance without notated music.

Incidental music   Music composed for performance in connection with a drama.

Instrumentation   The parts assigned to particular instruments in an ensemble.

Interval   The distance between two notes.

Jazz   A twentieth-century American musical style incorporating complex rhythms and improvisation.

Key   See *tonality*.

Largo   Very slow and broad tempo.

Legato   Smooth, connected style of performance.

Leitmotif   A motive or theme associated with a particular character or idea, used extensively by Richard Wagner.

Lento   Very slow.

Libretto   The text of an opera or oratorio

Lied   The German term for art song.

Madrigal   A secular work for small choir popular in the seventeenth century.

Major   One of the two basic scales used in Western music, see also *minor*.

Ma non troppo   A performance notation meaning "but not too much," used to qualify another term, as in *allegro ma non troppo*–"fast, but not too much."

Mass   The Roman Catholic Church's main service, frequently set to music (*Missa* in Latin).

Mazurka   A Polish dance in triple meter.

Measure   A group of beats set off in written music by vertical lines called bar lines.

Melody   A series of consecutive pitches with a recognizable shape or tune.

Meno   Means "less" in Italian.

Meter   The pattern created by stressed and unstressed beats.

Metronome   A device (mechanical or electrical) used to indicate the exact tempo of a composition.

Mezzo-soprano   A female voice with a range between a soprano and an alto.

Minor   One of the two basic scales in Western music, see also *major*.

Moderato   Moderate tempo.

Modes   Scale patterns derived from early church music that include major and minor.

Motive   A short melodic or rhythmic idea.

Movement   A large, independent section of an instrumental composition.

Music-drama   Wagner's term for his German operas.

Mute   A device for dampening and changing the tone of an instrument.

Neoclassical   A twentieth-centruy style that borrows compositional techniques from previus style periods.

Nocturne   A short, lyrical piano piece of the Romantic period that evokes feelings associated with the night.

Notes   Symbols written in musical notation to indicate pitches and rhythm.

Octave   An interval of eight pitches in which the first and last pitches have the same pitch name.

Octet   A work for eight performers.

Opera   A dramatic work, comedy or tragedy, set to music.

Operetta   A light opera with spoken dialogue.

Opus   Literally "work"; the number indicates the order in which the composer's works were written.

Oratorio   A large work for chorus, soloists, and orchestra usually on a religious topic; performed without scenery, costumes, or acting.

Orchestration   The art and technique of scoring music for an orchestra or group of instruments.

Ornament   One or more notes that embellish a melody.

Ostinato   A short, persistently repeated melodic or rhythmic figure.

Overture   An instrumental introduction to a larger work.

Phrase   A relatively short melodic statement similar to a clause or phrase or language.

Piano   (1) Keyboard instrument. (2) Quiet.

Pitch   The perceived highness or lowness of a musical sound, determined by the number of vibrations per second.

Pizzicato   A direction to string performers to pluck rather than bow the strings.

Poco   A performance direction meaning "little." For example, *poco accelerando* indicates "gradually play a little faster."

Polyphony   A texture in which two or more melodies of approximately equal importance occur at the same time.

Polyrhythm   Several different rhythmic patterns occurring at the same time.

Polytonality   Several tonalities present at the same time.

Prelude   (1) A short instrumental work usually played as an introduction to a larger work. (2) A short, independent instrumental work.

Presto   Very fast tempo.

Program music   Instrumental work descriptive of some nonmusical idea or object.

Program notes   Short descriptions or background information in the printed concert program about the music, the composer, and the performers.

Quartet   A work for four performers.

Quintet   A work for five performers.

Rallentando   Gradual slowing of tempo.

Recapitulation   The section of sonata form in which the themes from the exposition are heard again.

Recitative   A speechlike section found in operas, oratorios, cantatas, etc.

Requiem   The funeral Mass of the Roman Catholic Church.

Rhythm   The sensation of motion in music regulated by the duration and grouping of sounds.

Ritardando   Gradual slowing of the tempo.

Rococo   The highly ornamented style in music and the other arts prevalent in eighteenth-century European courts.

Rondo   A form in which the theme appears several times with contrasting sections between its appearances.

Rubato   A performer's slight deviation from strict rhythm for expressive effect.

Scale   A series of pitches that proceeds upward or downward according to a prescribed pattern.

Scherzo   (1) A lively movement usually in triple meter. (2) A self-contained piano piece.

Score   The complete notation of a work that includes a number of parts.

Secular music   Nonreligious music.

Sequence   The immediate repetition of a melodic idea using different pitches.

Serialism   A twentieth-century method of composing using tone rows and all twelve tones of the chromatic scale.

Sforzando   A loud, accented tone or chord.

Singspiel   German eighteenth-century opera with spoken dialogue.

Solo   A work in which one player or singer performs alone or is featured.

Sonata (1) A multimovement work for piano and another instrument, or for piano alone. (2) A Baroque piece for small instrumental ensemble.

Sonata form A large form consisting of an exposition section, followed by a development section and a recapitulation.

Song cycle A group of songs with a unifying theme.

Soprano The highest female voice or boy's voice.

Sprechstimme A vocal style combining speaking and singing.

Staccato A detached style of performing.

Suite (1) An instrumental work in several movements. (2) Portions of a larger work, such as a ballet or opera, performed as a group.

Symphonic poem Programmatic symphony in one movement, also called a tone poem.

Symphony An extended, multimovement orchestral work.

Syncopation Accented beats not normally expected within a particular meter.

Synthesizer An electronic instrument used to generate sounds.

Tempo The speed of the beats in a piece of music.

Tenor A male voice higher than baritone or bass.

Texture The way in which the individual parts of music are layered and woven.

Theme The main melody or melodies in a piece of music.

Timbre Tone quality or color.

Toccata A display piece for a keyboard instrument.

Tonality A key or tonal center.

Tone poem See *Symphonic poem.*

Tone-row music (twelve-tone) See *serialism.*

Tonic (key center) The specific pitch around which a piece of music is centered.

Tonic chord A chord built on the first pitch of a major or minor scale.

Transcription   An adaptation of a musical work for a different instrument, voice, or ensemble.

Transposition   A piece or section of music written or performed at a pitch other than the original one.

Triad   A chord consisting of three pitches usually separated by intervals of thirds.

Trill   A musical ornament consisting of rapid alternations of two tones

Tutti   An Italian performance term indicating that the entire ensemble plays.

Twelve-tone music   See *serialism.*

Unison   Performing the same pitches or melody at the same time.

Variation   A section of music in which the melody, harmony, or rhythm of a theme is repeated with some changes.

Vibrato   A rapid fluctuation of pitch or pulsation of tone for expressiveness.

Virtuoso   A technically skilled performer.

Vivace   Very fast, lively tempo.

Whole-tone scale   A scale in which the octave is divided into six whole steps.

Wind ensemble   A wind instrument band smaller than the traditional band.

INDEX